ATTACK DOG MARKETING

ATTACK DOG MARKETING

Take a bite out of your small business's competition

JEB BREITHAUPT AND SCOTT WYSONG

Copyright © 2017 Jeb Breithaupt & Scott Wysong
All rights reserved.

ISBN-13: 9781548005283
ISBN-10: 1548005282

TABLE OF CONTENTS

Introduction · ix

Chapter 1 Does Your Dog Bite? · **1**
    Jeb's Gems· 2
    Scott's Steps· 4
    The Marketing and Sales Link · · · · · · · · · · · 8
    Do You Bark? · 9

Chapter 2 My Dog Ate My Homework · · · · · · · · · · · · · · · · · · · **11**
    Jeb's Gems· ·12
    Scott's Steps· ·14
    The Marketing and Sales Link · · · · · · · · · · · ·17
    Do You Bark? ·17

Chapter 3 You *Can* Teach an Old Dog New Tricks · · · · · · · · · · · · · · · **19**
    Jeb's Gems· 20
    Scott's Steps· 22
    The Marketing and Sales Link · · · · · · · · · · · ·31
    Do You Bark? ·31

Chapter 4 The Sniff Test · **33**
    Jeb's Gems· 34
    Scott's Steps· 36

	The Marketing and Sales Link	42
	Do You Bark?	42
Chapter 5	**The Tail Wagging the Dog**	**43**
	Jeb's Gems	44
	Scott's Steps	45
	The Marketing and Sales Link	49
	Do You Bark?	50
Chapter 6	**Barking up the Wrong Tree**	**51**
	Jeb's Gems	52
	Scott's Steps	53
	The Marketing and Sales Link	59
	Do You Bark?	60
Chapter 7	**Throw Me a Bone**	**61**
	Jeb's Gems	62
	Scott's Steps	63
	The Marketing and Sales Link	69
	Do You Bark?	70
Chapter 8	**The Lead Dog**	**71**
	Jeb's Gems	72
	Scott's Steps	75
	The Marketing and Sales Link	83
	Do You Bark?	83
Chapter 9	**Your Dog and Pony Show**	**85**
	Jeb's Gems	87
	Scott's Steps	89
	The Marketing and Sales Link	98
	Do You Bark?	99
Chapter 10	**Meaner than a Junkyard Dog**	**101**
	Jeb's Gems	102
	Scott's Steps	104
	The Marketing and Sales Link	109
	Do You Bark?	109

Chapter 11 Every Dog Has Its Day ··························· ·111
    Jeb's Gems· ··112
    Scott's Steps· ·······································113
    The Marketing and Sales Link ······················119
    Do You Bark? ····································· ·120

Epilogue That Dog Will Hunt ····················· 121

INTRODUCTION

A ton of business books focus on marketing. Yet, few of them are specifically about small-business marketing. And even fewer speak directly to small-business owners.

This one does.

Too many small-business owners believe only big businesses have brand equity, customer surveys, advertising or a customer bill of rights. The fact is, no matter how small your business is, you can have those things, too. You *should* have those things, too.

That's why we wrote this book. We wanted to offer small businesses a straightforward approach to marketing. And because marketing is an effort that requires input and action from the employees of those small businesses, as well as from the owner and manager, we wanted to write a book that would be relevant to every small-business staff member.

In a small business, it's "all hands on deck," even when it comes to marketing.

Attack Dog Marketing is an easy read. Take it along on your next flight. Enjoy the stories about the successes and challenges that the owner and employees of JEB Design/Build have had on the high-end remodeling firm's way to the top of its market. Learn from a marketing professor's perspective on the best way to create your brand, market your products and services, and sell whatever you make or do.

This book has two authors with very different backgrounds. Yet both of them are on the same page—pun intended—when it comes to marketing.

In each chapter, small-business owner and consultant Jeb Breithaupt introduces some marketing concepts with relevant and specific examples and stories from his 30 plus years of owning and running his remodeling company in Shreveport, Louisiana. Even though his firm has only 11 employees, Jeb is successful doing many of the things in marketing that the "big dogs" are doing.

Long-time college professor Scott Wysong shares the experiences, from the classroom and the field, that he and his students have had as they worked on projects with real firms as consultants.

We recognize that each industry, and company, for that matter, is different. So you may think some of our examples, stories, keys and even quotes are not applicable to you. Most of them are. We challenge you to think about how you are currently marketing and how you could improve it based on the concepts in each chapter.

In fact, in each chapter, we've included some questions and keys that we call BARK. Our BARK model is composed of four processes to help you organize your thoughts on marketing.

The first process is to **brainstorm**. While everyone is familiar with the idea, few companies truly encourage brainstorming among their teams and employees. Brainstorming is most successful in businesses that embrace a corporate culture of open dialogue and thinking "outside the box."

The truth is most people don't want to think "outside the box." For one, it takes creativity and time. Second, people are often afraid that their ideas will be laughed at or rejected. So it's just easier to keep quiet and do things "the way we've always done them around here."

Brainstorming leads to marketing changes that work because it invites everyone to consider all possible options and to accept that no idea is bad or outrageous. Now, if you are the small-business owner, this is going to take patience and an open mind. If you created everything from the company name to its logo to the price structure to your customer service policies, you're very likely to feel defensive when an employee who has been with you for less than a year starts questioning things. We've seen it hundreds of times.

Thinking differently about the company's marketing is like calling somebody's kid ugly. It can cause tension unless everyone, including the owner, welcomes new ideas. And remember, these are just ideas. You don't have to implement them. Just consider them.

The second process is the **assessment**. This is an analysis that helps you look at what you are doing to currently market your business and its products or services.

The third process is to **rank** your thoughts or concepts.

In the last process, we tell you the **key things** you need to do in order to keep your current customers and acquire new ones. Once again, instead of quickly dismissing our keys to implement, think about how each key could be tailored to fit your company.

The BARK model is very simple, but we think it will help everyone at a small business think and discuss the company's marketing.

We also included in each chapter a section called "The Marketing and Sales Link" that discusses how salespeople can use some of the marketing concepts in their selling. As we discuss in Chapter 1, there is no reason to have sales and marketing disconnected in your company (big or small).

We hope that you not only enjoy our book, but that it helps your small business. We both are very passionate about marketing and want to see you become an Attack Dog Marketer!

Jeb Breithaupt, B. Arch., MBA is the president of JEB Design/Build, a second-generation remodeling company in Shreveport, Louisiana, and of JEB Marketing, a consulting firm specializing in marketing and sales coaching for remodelers, builders and home-improvement contractors. Jeb's company ranks in the top tier of remodelers based on profit margins. He is often quoted in construction industry trade publications and in news stories. He writes a weekly column for homeowners on home-improvement topics for the *Shreveport Times*, has written for *remodeling* magazine, and blogs for *BUILDER* magazine.

Scott Wysong, Ph.D. is an associate professor of marketing in the Satish & Yasmin Gupta College of Business at the University of Dallas. Prior to academia, Scott worked for almost 10 years as the head of the operational audit department for a hospital system evaluating the expenses, staffing and productivity in every department of the hospital, its clinics and its fitness center. He continues to work as a consultant with firms in sports, healthcare, oil and gas and others. He has worked as a marketing consultant with more than 100 firms.

CHAPTER 1
DOES YOUR DOG BITE?

Developing a plan of attack on your competitors

JEB'S GEMS
    *   It's Time to Bite Back
SCOTT'S STEPS
    *   Defending Your Turf and Hunting for Prey
    *   Skip Knows Marketing and Sales. Do You?
    *   Marketing: Simply Defined
    *   Why Should Someone Buy From You?
THE MARKETING AND SALES LINK
DO YOU BARK?

> *"Businesses will do better in the end if they concentrate on meeting customers' needs rather than on selling products."*
>
> —THEODORE LEVITT
> PROFESSOR EMERITUS, HARVARD UNIVERSITY

JEB'S GEMS
IT'S TIME TO BITE BACK

The great fallacy of the Great American Dream is the notion that if you get up early, show up for work every day and do the best job you can—maybe better than anyone—you'll be a great success.

The fact is that you need to do all of that *plus* marketing.

You can be a superb craftsman, a whiz with numbers, a brilliant lawyer or a master chef, but your small business will fail if nobody knows why it's special or that it even exists.

You have to tell your story—to the world.

Possessing great talent and doing superior work don't necessarily equal success. Lots of smart, passionate, highly skilled remodelers, builders, architects, plumbers, painters and carpenters struggle to make a living, despite their "awesomeness." For that matter, so do a lot of self-employed accountants, lawyers, cooks and veterinarians.

Don't fall into the trap of believing that just because you do good work and love what you do, the money will come. Instead, *market your business.*

That's what your competition is doing, and their phones are ringing. That's where your potential customers are shopping for the services that you can do better. Your marketing-savvy competitors are taking a bite out of your success.

It's time for you to bite back.

Marketing your business will put you in the fight—and that's what business is: a fight, a competition for clients and their money.

You might have thought your business was about home-improvement or house painting or deck-building.

That's your *craft*. In *Attack Dog Marketing*, we're talking about *business*.

I consult with a lot of remodelers and builders, and I haven't seen a single one take off without a solid marketing effort, an *Attack Dog Marketing* effort.

Don't panic; I'm not going to send you out like the old "tin man" salesmen to knock on doors, talk your way into the homes of strangers and then go in for the kill, refusing to leave until the homeowner signs on the dotted line.

That's selling by bullying, and it doesn't work.

Attack Dog Marketing isn't selling. It's about taking a bite out of your competition by telling everyone and anyone who might be in the market for the services or products you offer that you've got them and that yours are better than anyone's. It's about attracting new customers and keeping the ones you have so they'll give you repeat business.

Marketing has two important functions: It helps you capture the interest of a potential customer, and it prepares that prospect to do business with your company.

Marketing is different from selling; it's different from advertising. Marketing lets the people who eventually will buy something from you know that you exist; what's special about your product or service, what your company is all about and why it's the best one in the neighborhood.

Marketing makes selling 100 percent easier. You set up sales through marketing. In other words, marketing is your pre-sales effort.

Marketing will help you find prospective customers by making it easy for them to find you. It also will help you "qualify" those would-be customers by filtering out people who aren't a good fit for your business.

Before you balk at turning away potential clients, stay with me for a second.

If you're a high-end home remodeler who specializes in kitchen overhauls and room additions—like I do—you're wasting your valuable time and the time of a customer who comes to you looking for a handyman to hang a heavy mirror in the bedroom or replace a few cracked floor tiles in the foyer.

Do your marketing right, and the "right" customers will find you. The homeowner with a $300 job for hire will filter herself out if she knows you do only large remodeling projects and not Mr. Fix-It work.

Marketing is a process of filtering, and it's a process of educating the client. It gets the prospect—the right prospect—on the phone or in the door to talk to you or your salesperson or your manager.

It lays the foundation for a quicker and easier sale because the customer already knows that your company does what she needs. She already has a pretty good idea of the price ranges you work in—and if she can afford you. She's already impressed with what she's heard or seen about your company's history, staff, customer service policy and craftsmanship.

Marketing makes the sale yours to lose. With priming like that, you'd have to work pretty hard to lose it.

Still, most small-business owners don't want to take the time or spend the money for this up-front, pre-sales marketing work. Some still have pre-recession visions of the "good old days" when customers lined up around the corner for the chance to buy what you had to sell, when business owners were taking orders faster than they could fill them, and when marketing was barely necessary.

That was then.

Today, you have to do *something* to find leads, turn them into prospects and convince them to close the deal. That something is marketing.

SCOTT'S STEPS
DEFENDING YOUR TURF AND HUNTING FOR PREY

Attack Dog Marketers are proactive in marketing—thinking of ways to improve their companies' marketing *every day*. They are relentless in questioning anything and everything with regard to their marketing. They do whatever they can—legally and ethically—to protect their small business.

I think too many firms focus on getting new customers or finding new revenue streams at the expense of taking care of and keeping their existing customers. (We'll talk more about this in Chapter 7). So to be an Attack Dog Marketer, you have to defend your turf and hunt for prey.

The Attack Dog Marketing Checklist

1. Defend Your Turf (Keep your current customers!)
2. Hunt for Prey (Look for new customers!)

In the classic movie, *The Pink Panther Strikes Again*, actor Peter Sellers, who plays the clumsy Inspector Clouseau, asks a German hotelier, "Does your dog bite?" as he points at the small dog in the lobby. The hotelier replies, "No." Yet, as Clouseau reaches down to pet the dog, the dog bites his hand.

"I thought you said your dog does not bite," Clouseau angrily demands. "I did," the German calmly replies. "That's not my dog."

Obviously, Clouseau's assumption hurt him. Similarly, many small-business owners assume that they don't have to do marketing or that they can't afford it. Not true.

Every firm can and should have a marketing plan and actually use the plan to make decisions—instead of just reaching out and getting bit!

Marketing is not just about advertising or sales. It is a mindset that needs to be embraced by everyone in the organization. Without marketing, there are no customers. Without customers, there's no revenue. And without any money, of course, the business closes.

Motivational speaker and author Larry Winget often says that the customer is our boss, and that we all work for our customers. This is never more true than in a small business. While large firms and government agencies may get funding from stockholders and tax dollars, the small business relies on the people who buy its products or services.

In today's business world, very few, if any, companies can say they have no competition. They may think they "own" their market, but the odds are good that plenty of other companies are looking to take away their customers every chance they get. As the Internet lowers the barriers to entry into almost every kind of business, a graphic design agency in Dallas may wind up competing with a teenager in the Czech Republic who has the same software.

In the case of a small business, you've got competitors on both ends of the spectrum. On one end, the Big Box retailers and Fortune 500 firms have the capital and economies of scale that make them difficult to challenge. On the other end is a growing group of competitors I call the "garage entrepreneurs." They bake cakes in their own kitchen, fix cars on the side, sell nutritional supplements out of the trunk of their car—you name it. They are selling the same product or service as you, but without the overhead.

That brings us back to marketing. If you want to compete, you've got to market. While you may have read that some firms like Starbucks spent very little on advertising in their initial years, that doesn't mean they didn't market.

As we will discuss throughout this book, marketing includes assessing your business environment, setting goals, researching your customers, delivering a high level of customer service, creating a strong brand identity and setting the right price.

SKIP KNOWS MARKETING AND SALES. DO YOU?

I have had a number of dogs over the years, and agree with the "dog whisperer" Cesar Millan and other experts who have observed that most dogs just want a simple, structured life. In my opinion, marketing is the same way. It's not that complex, *if* you have a structured plan.

As we mentioned in the Introduction, Jeb and I have written this book with the intent of being very simple and straightforward. That way, you can implement some of the concepts and strategies in your business as you read each chapter. But you've got to take action. Simply reading the book and saying to yourself, "That made sense, but I don't have time to market" won't do you any good.

Years ago, I assigned the MBA students in a marketing class to work on teams to develop a marketing plan for a real firm. One of the teams of students was assigned to develop a plan for a sports franchise that I had lined up as the students' client. I knew several of the students on this team from previous classes, and considered them good students who understood the concepts of marketing. Yet, they couldn't ever get around to "pulling the trigger" on this project.

It turns out they were afraid to send the client a survey they created to give to the team's fans to answer because they worried the client wouldn't like it. They were hesitant to make any kind of bold recommendations that could upset the client. They constantly asked me for more time on their deadlines and routinely indicated that they needed more information before making a decision.

Fed up, I finally said to them, "Look, business decisions aren't made with unlimited time and perfect information. At some point, you just have to make a decision."

Then I told them, "I think my dog, Skip, could have completed this project by now."

While they probably found the canine comparison less than endearing, they went on to construct an excellent plan that really pleased the client. In fact, the client actually didn't like some of the recommendations, but understood how the team of students justified them. To this day, those students say they are thankful they were forced to make a decision on their project. And of course, they always ask how Skip is doing.

Hopefully, you'll make some marketing decisions for your business based on this book.

MARKETING: SIMPLY DEFINED

Everyone has heard the term "marketing." Heck, we've already mentioned the term a number of times so far in Chapter 1. Still, it's worth taking a step back and asking yourself, "What is the purpose of marketing?"

Of course, we want to sell things. But how do we do that? The answer is simple: Marketing enables a company **to meet a customer's needs**. It's a very basic definition, but it's true. The trick to successful marketing is finding out what consumers need and want.

Marketing is so important that it has gone from not really even being a discipline or academic major only 40 years ago to occupying such an important place in business today. Unlike chemistry or physics, marketing has no defined formulas for accomplishing the challenging task of trying to understand and predict human behavior. So marketing uses concepts from economics, sociology, anthropology, psychology, communication and statistics to try to better understand why people buy what they buy.

WHY SHOULD SOMEONE BUY FROM YOU?

A term that marketers often use is called **differential advantage**. Sometimes, they refer to it as **competitive advantage** or **sustainable competitive**

advantage. No matter what you call it, it means determining how your firm is truly different from others—especially your competitors.

Many new businesses fail each year. While every new business faces an uphill battle because it starts off with little brand awareness among the public, very little capital, a high learning curve for the owner and new staff, and other hurdles, the biggest reason that new businesses fail is because they don't differentiate themselves. They don't tell their potential customers why their product or service is different from the ones those consumers are already using.

Simply being a "me too" or copycat company that has a different logo from everyone else or undercuts the market in price is not sustainable. There aren't too many McDowell's today—the McDonald's knockoff in the 80's comedy classic movie, *Coming to America*.

THE MARKETING AND SALES LINK

As we will see later in the book, **personal selling** is a tool that a firm can use to communicate with potential customers and to promote itself. Many firms, big and small, hire a salesperson or sales team and tell them to sell, sell, sell. Yet, they seem to forget the basic concepts of marketing that will aid them in their selling.

Worse yet is the firm that says to the salespeople, "Your job is to sell. Let the marketing department do the marketing." How can you have marketing and sales departments that don't work together? I've seen that model at many companies, but I've never seen it work out.

Consider a former MBA student of mine whose day job was in sales at a Fortune 500 telecom company. After class each week, she would ask me for advice on "how to handle" her marketing department. It seems the marketing department would place ads in trade journals and run special pricing and promotions, but never even tell—much less discuss—these decisions with the sales department. So when she and the other salespeople went into the field every day to meet with clients, they had no knowledge—or answers—about the pricing and promotions. Needless to say, it made for a very tense work environment.

My advice: The two departments have to work together. It's that simple.

DO YOU BARK?

Brainstorm:
- How are you making your customers' lives better?

Assess:
- Who in the organization has input in marketing and sales decisions?
- Is the group of decision-makers too big or too small?

Rank:
- If you could only ask your customers *one* question, what would it be?

Keys to Implement:

<u>Attack Dog Key to Defend Your Turf</u>:
Share your marketing plan with all of your employees within the next month.

<u>Attack Dog Key to Hunt Your Prey</u>:
Ask every employee for one new marketing idea within the next month.

CHAPTER 2
MY DOG ATE MY HOMEWORK

Why having a written plan with specific goals is so important

JEB'S GEMS
    *   Get with the 'Program'
SCOTT'S STEPS
    *   Your Firm's Values and Culture
    *   The Mission Statement
    *   Creating SMART Objectives
THE MARKETING AND SALES LINK
DO YOU BARK?

"Control your own destiny or someone else will."

—JACK WELCH
FORMER CEO OF GENERAL ELECTRIC

JEB'S GEMS
GET WITH THE 'PROGRAM'

This chapter is all about how important it is for small-business owners like you and me to create a marketing plan and write it down.

I know you don't want to; neither did I at first.

Most small-business owners don't *really* want to do any of the stuff they have to do to keep their businesses operating in the black. We're busy, busy, busy. We want to spend our time practicing our craft, whatever that may be.

Since I hung a shingle for JEB Design/Build in 1983, my passion has been designing homes and remodeling kitchens and bathrooms. Maybe yours is building houses or repairing them. Another small-business owner's might be designing fashions, cooking gourmet meals, repairing bicycles or healing sick pets.

People like us want to do what we love and what we're good at, not write a bunch of plans.

The truth is, if you want to continue to practice your craft, you need to get paid to do it. In order to get paid, you need to find some qualified buyers. To find the buyers, you need to market your business.

So marketing really is nothing short of a survival skill.

You can do that marketing without a formal, written plan; lots of sole proprietors do. They figure they've got it all in their heads. Or, they don't really know what they want to do or don't want to commit to a specific specialty, so the thought of writing a plan feels like too great of a commitment.

But here's what happens the minute they hire even one employee: That employee, left without any specific instructions about how you want to run your shop, portray yourself to the public or build your specialty, probably won't do things the way you had in mind.

The reason: He or she can't *read* your mind.

The employee can, however, read your marketing plan. If your plan is a good one, it will include a statement that explains your mission and vision for the company. It will outline the company's core values. And every employee you bring on board needs to know what those are, and buy into them, and agree to live by them.

Seems like writing that down might be smart, doesn't it?

Most employees appreciate working for an entrepreneur with a mighty passion for the work. They want to be invested in that. If you live and breathe your passion, they're more likely to do the same.

That's great, and it can work on an informal basis, especially at a very small company.

But here's what happens as the company grows: Employees learn the company's culture from each other instead of from you. They teach each other the "program," so they know what to do and say to get ahead. The grapevine lets them know how to get a raise and avoid being fired. The day-to-day replaces the passion. And you're too busy to be a cheerleader.

Before you know it, the culture looks completely different from the one in your vision.

A document that outlines the owner's vision for the company's success, reputation, customer service and other areas that make up a business's culture can serve as a guiding star for your employees—and as a reminder to you when things get hectic.

You see, marketing begins within the company. Every successful marketing effort has at its foundation a staff—no matter how small—that understands the owner's vision well enough to carry it out, even when the owner isn't around.

At JEB Design/Build, for instance, our culture dictates that every phone call is important. It's so important, in fact, that I hung a sign in the office to remind my staff to "answer the doggone phone before the fourth ring." Letting a call go to voice mail is not allowed. Nobody in that office—from the designers to the draftsmen to the bookkeeper—thinks for a minute that it isn't his or her job to answer that doggone phone.

That simple, written policy has put a lot of money in my pocket.

Not too long ago when the office phone rang, a guy on my staff, who probably thought he was too busy to pick it up, answered it anyway because he knew better than to let it ring too long. The homeowner on the other end of that phone call hired us for a $1.4 million new home.

I'll bet you some busy guy who works for my competitor would have let it go to voice mail. Maybe he did, and that's why I got the call.

That's a marketing plan at work. It works because every employee knows it and follows it. It's a written document. It's discussed at every staff meeting, not just marketing meetings. I even made a bunch of videos based on my marketing plan—starring yours truly—and I encourage my team to watch them over and over.

That way, nobody has to guess what I want. Everybody *knows* the company's goal is to design and execute large-scale home remodeling projects. Everybody can *explain* that to anyone who asks. And everybody *knows better* than to pursue customers who are looking just for plumbing repairs or quick paint jobs.

Here's what I tell remodelers and builders when they ask me to help them rev up their sales and marketing effort: Even if you just can't bring yourself to write your marketing plan down, talk about it with your employees every chance you get. Every detail of it should be automatic for your employees. Executing it every day should be what your company's culture is about.

If you're ready to formalize your process, read on. Scott's got some step-by-step advice for getting started.

SCOTT'S STEPS
YOUR FIRM'S VALUES AND CULTURE

As you write your marketing plan, start with your company values. What values define your business? Honesty, hard work, pride in craftsmanship and respect for others? What else do you value? Which are most important?

Successful companies make their core values part of their culture. 3M has a culture of innovation. Whole Foods is green. Zappos' culture is all about customer service.

Of course, a lot of companies say they value innovation, green initiatives and customers. But these three actually walk the talk. When Zappos CEO Tony Hsieh founded the company, for example, he didn't know anything about shoes. He had been successful in the information technology field, and he knew that if he put the customer first, he could sell anything. To create his culture of the customer, he started from scratch. Hundreds of applicants with many years of experience in "customer service" for telecom, cable TV and electricity firms applied for jobs with him. "No thanks," Tony said.

Instead, he wanted friendly people who liked to help others. He didn't want all of the experienced service or sales reps from other firms that claimed to be about the customer, but weren't.

A company's values drive its culture, and that starts at the top. If the employees don't see the company owner or CEO embracing the values, why should they?

THE MISSION STATEMENT

In my hometown of Fort Worth, Texas, there is a popular barbecue place called The Railhead. Above the bar is a simple sign that says "WYBMABIITY." Locals often bring attention to the sign when an unsuspecting out-of-towner orders a beer, and the conversation goes something like this:

"Can you guess what that sign stands for?" a local will ask.

When the out-of-towner says, "I don't know," the local replies, "Will you buy me a beer if I tell you?"

The out-of-towner reluctantly agrees. "Sure. So what does it stand for?"

"Will you buy me a beer if I tell you?" the local repeats.

"I said I would. What does it stand for?" the out-of-towner demands, becoming more agitated as all the locals listen in on the prank.

This goes on for a few rounds until the annoyed out-of-towner catches on that "WYBMABIITY" stands for, "Will you buy me a beer if I tell you?"

While it's not the classic Laurel and Hardy "Who's on first?" routine, you get the point. Whenever I ask people what their firm's mission statement is (and offer to buy them a beer if they can tell me), few, if any, know it word for word. In fact, few can even paraphrase it. And some can't even guess.

It shouldn't be that tough. The mission statement should be a simple statement that *every* employee can recite from memory.

If you were to look at the mission statements of some Fortune 500 firms—with the companies' names omitted—you might be hard pressed to figure out to which firms they belong. For example, whose mission statement is this?

* To refresh the world
* To inspire moments of optimism and happiness
* To create value and make a difference

This is Coca-Cola's mission statement. It's short—which is a plus—but it is vague. To be fair, a corporate vision statement that goes along with the mission statement lists the importance of the company's people, profits and other important issues. But the mission is still too broad, in my opinion.

A mission statement shouldn't be too narrow either. In his famous 1960 essay, "Marketing Myopia," former Harvard Professor Theodore Levitt implores business owners to think beyond their current products and markets. He gives the example of the railroads. Levitt asserted that the railroads would still be thriving today if they had defined their business as "transportation" instead of "railroads." When the railroads were booming, they didn't look ahead to the future, viewing only other railroad firms as their competition and ignoring the emergence of trucks and airplanes as other ways to transport goods and people.

As we discussed in Chapter 1, a business's main focus should be on meeting customer needs. Those needs change over time. So looking at your customers' needs now and in the future is very important. Recognizing that you might have completely different customers or markets in the future is vital, as well.

While you want the mission statement to be optimistic so it will instill a sense of pride in both your employees and your customers, it still needs to be realistic. If you can strike that balance, you'll get a mission statement that employees can buy into … and remember.

CREATING SMART OBJECTIVES

Like some mission statements, marketing objectives or goals can be too general. Instead of setting an objective "to make our customers happy," you could strive to "have a satisfactory rating of 90 percent or above on our self-developed customer service scale each year." This is **specific, measurable, attainable,**

relevant and **time-bound**—or **SMART**. Other SMART measures to include in your business's marketing objectives could be total sales, percent of sales from existing/new customers, sales per customer, market share (in units sold and dollars sold), unique visitors to your company's Web site, Web page click-through rates, the amount of time each visitor spends on your Web page, the customer's intent to purchase, and the percentage of customers who are aware of and loyal to your brand.

For any goal or objective that you identify for the first time, you are really just making an educated guess as to how likely you will be able to meet it. Yet, over time, you should be able to refine your objectives so they are more and more attainable—with gradual increases each year. We'll talk more about measuring whether you met your objectives—or not—in Chapter 11.

THE MARKETING AND SALES LINK

It is important that the salesperson's objectives are aligned with the company's marketing objectives. A number of years ago, I had a student who was a sales representative for a Fortune 500 technology firm. The company had set corporate objectives to really push its new software. However, the sales staff still got a significantly higher commission for selling the old software. Which one do you think they sold? Getting input from the sales department on the objectives early on may have averted this disconnect.

DO YOU BARK?

Brainstorm:
- * If you had to condense your mission statement down to five words, what would it say?

Assess:
- * How often do you review your marketing plan? Create a formal process and timeline to periodically review it.

<u>R</u>ank:
* If you had to pick one, what would be your company's core value?

<u>K</u>eys to Implement:

<u>Attack Dog Key to Defend Your Turf</u>:
Make 90 percent customer satisfaction an objective now.

<u>Attack Dog Key to Hunt Your Prey</u>:
Grow your sales by 10 percent this year.

CHAPTER 3
YOU *CAN* TEACH AN OLD DOG NEW TRICKS

Using marketing research to make informed decisions

JEB'S GEMS
* You're Already Doing Market Research

SCOTT'S STEPS
* Primary vs. Secondary Research
* Collecting the Data
* Designing a Survey
* The Right Sample Size?
* How to Use the Results

THE MARKETING AND SALES LINK

DO YOU BARK?

> *"Advertising people who ignore research are as dangerous as generals who ignore decodes of enemy signals."*
>
> —DAVID OGILVY
> FOUNDER OF OGILVY & MATHER ADVERTISING AGENCY

JEB'S GEMS
YOU'RE ALREADY DOING MARKET RESEARCH

Before you say you don't have the time or money to invest in market research, consider this: You're already doing it.

Say you own a building or remodeling company, like I do. When your lumber dealer tells you that your competitor has started designing kitchens, as well as building them, and you remember that your last prospect told you she would rather work with a company that does both of those things instead of with your company, which only builds, that's market research. If you drive past three of that competitor's yard signs in one neighborhood, and then you look up his Web site and see a big discount for customers who buy both design and building services, you're doing market research. And that log you keep in your head of how many of your recent prospects wanted some design help from you or at least asked for a referral to a designer? That's market research.

Just because you didn't key any of that information into a spreadsheet doesn't mean it's not valuable or that you can't use it to shore up your sales effort, tweak your prices or even make a wholesale change to your business model by adding interior design or another service that your gut is telling you is in high demand.

Likewise, you might not know exactly how many prospects asked you about kitchens last month compared with how many wanted bathrooms or room additions, but you know if it was more or fewer. Did you write it down? No. But if you had, that would be called market research.

You're already doing market research—on a very simple scale—even if you don't call it that. So why not harness the information that you're already collecting into something just a little bit more formal? Once you write this "data" down and organize it, it will help you keep track of the trends you're already picking up on, which could lead you to offer specials or focus any advertising you do on whatever is trending in your area.

Or, when you're getting ready to build a spec home, that documentation will remind you that at last year's Parade of Homes, two-thirds of the 80 people you talked to said they wanted a media room more than a formal dining room or that almost everyone indicated a preference for Tuscan-style architecture, for example. You can use that insight to decide which of those to include in the house.

Formalize it. Write it down. Take advantage of the power of the market research you're already doing.

At JEB Design/Build, we write everything down. We take thorough notes during every meeting with every prospect anyway, so it doesn't really cost us anything more to keep a running tally of how many of them said they wanted new exterior doors, or renovated kitchens, or updated bathrooms. We keep a list of which size windows people ask for and whether they want granite or quartz countertops. With that information about current homeowner preferences in hand, we know which products and services to include in our ads for the month. We know which hot sellers to suggest to prospects and clients as we talk to them about their home-improvement projects.

We leverage the informal market research we do every day into a program that's a little bit more formalized and a lot more useful than just keeping it in our heads.

Write it down and watch the trends reveal themselves to you. Two examples from our shop:

1. We count the number of homes in our local Parade of Homes every year. So when we noticed a 23 percent increase in a single year after several years of flat or dwindling participation that gave us a lot of information. It told us the market was finally rebounding, and that people have more money to spend on remodeling. As a result, we started suggesting larger and higher-end projects when we talked with prospects.
2. We track the number of leads we get and the potential value of each of those prospects' projects. A few years ago, our numbers told us that although we were getting way more leads than we had just a few months prior, they were for small projects, like door replacements. We want bigger projects, so we changed our advertising and even what we talk about when people ask us about our business. Now, we talk about kitchen renovations and room additions.

The bottom line: Your gut and your memory are good tools, but a written record is better. As the old Chinese proverb says, "The palest ink is better than the best memory."

SCOTT'S STEPS
PRIMARY VS. SECONDARY RESEARCH

Marketing research is all about data, and there are two main types of data collection: primary and secondary. **Primary research** is brand-new information that you collect—or hire a marketing firm to collect for you—for the first time. You can get this data by surveying your customers, for example. We'll come back to this later in the chapter.

Secondary research is data that you can use, but that someone else has already collected. The U. S. Census Bureau, for example, collects information about how many people live in different cities and states, how much money they earn, how big their families are and so on. You might use Census data to find out more about the people who live near your business as you plan where to focus your marketing effort or how much to charge for a product.

Nielsen, another source of secondary research, is a firm that collects information on which TV shows people are watching, which Web sites they visit, what radio stations they listen to and which movies they watch, for example. Nielsen also is very involved in collecting what is called scanner or point of sale (POS) data, which I will explain later in this chapter. Many trade associations also provide research information about their members and their customers. These are just a few examples of secondary research.

The biggest advantage of secondary research is that you can obtain the results far cheaper than you can collect primary research on your own. Some secondary research is free; government research from the Census Bureau and other agencies is often available to everyone at no charge. Nielsen and other private research organizations charge for their information. Even so, it is less expensive than if you had to collect it yourself.

A problem with secondary research is that it's not always relevant or timely. If you're in the tech or telecom industry, for example, a study from six months ago may not be timely enough for you, and it may cover overall industry matters instead of specifically addressing issues that affect your company.

Because of this, professional marketers also use primary research. It is data collected for the very first time, making it relevant and timely. Collecting it still takes time, and it can be very expensive to do: A marketing firm may charge you anywhere from $5,000 to $500,000 on up, depending on the information you want to obtain. Most businesses try to use a mixture of primary and secondary research to gather information.

COLLECTING THE DATA

If you choose to conduct primary research to collect your marketing research data—either on your own or through a marketing company—you have several formats from which to choose.

1. **Observation.** As we learned from Jeb's remodeling company examples earlier in this chapter, if you watch what your customers do, and then think about why they do it, you can gain insight into their reasons for buying from you. For instance, every time you visit a grocery store, it collects a ton of information about your purchase, even if you don't have a loyalty card.

    By scanning the bar code on the back of the product, the store knows what was bought, when it was bought, if it was on sale, whether a coupon was used and its location within the store. A lot of observation goes on that the public often does not realize is happening.

2. **Mystery shoppers.** Another form of marketing observation includes mystery shoppers—people who go "undercover" by posing as shoppers, and then report their findings to the company that hired them. You might send a mystery shopper into the business of a competitor to learn its prices and sales pitches. Or you could send one into your own business to get a report about how well your employees treated the "customer." A lot of restaurants do this, and department stores,

health care providers and even airlines now hire mystery shoppers, as well.

3. **Experimentation** is another marketing tool. You probably took a class in physics or chemistry or biology in school, where you conducted experiments. Marketers do the same thing. In an experiment, marketers control as many variables as possible and manipulate only one or two in order to see how they influence customers. The two basic types of experiments in marketing are lab experiments and field experiments.

In **lab experiments**, marketers bring people into a facility and have them try out different products and services.

For example, consumers may taste three cups of new soft drinks that are labeled A, B and C. The temperature of the soft drinks is kept the same, and they are all in the same kind of cup. The experiment measures which of these three soft drinks people prefer, all other factors being equal.

A problem is that lab experiments are very high in control, but low in realism. To get realism, marketers also use **field experiments**, which is when the actual product is sold in a test market. Test markets are cities where the new product is placed on store shelves to see if people will actually buy it, and how often. Cities like Wichita Falls, Texas; Akron, Ohio; and Lacrosse, Wisconsin, are popular test markets because they are moderately large cities, but not so big that marketers cannot manipulate some of the variables, like advertising, pricing and shelf location. This means that they are high in realism, but lower in control. To strike a balance between realism and control, marketers often use both lab and field experiments before they actually launch a product (You can bet that Coke wished they did some field testing before they lost tens of millions on the New Coke launch in the 1980's, which some consider to be one of the biggest marketing research blunders in history.).

4. **Surveys.** Here are the most popular kinds of surveys that businesses use to collect data:
    * Paper-based **mail surveys** go to customers' homes and are sometimes targeted to a postal code, city or state. Respondents can answer at their leisure, and they feel more anonymous. A problem with mail surveys is that people don't always complete them because they consider them junk mail or they intend to complete them, but ultimately procrastinate and fail to do so. And because the company issuing the survey cannot clarify the questions for the respondents, the questions have to be very clear.
    * **E-mail surveys** are cheap and easy to send, and the data is compiled instantly into a database when you use a service like SurveyMonkey.com. Their biggest weakness is that spam filters and out-of-date e-mail addresses can keep the surveys from finding their way to potential respondents. Plus, if an e-mail survey is set up improperly, respondents can fill it out multiple times if they choose to, leading to inaccurate data. The e-mail survey is still a powerful and economical tool, if it is used properly.
    * **Phone surveys** used to be popular and are still occasionally done today. They are harder to execute because of the increased prevalence of caller ID service. If someone does agree to take a phone survey, it has to be quick and short because respondents are not going to spend a lot of time with you on the phone. The greatest advantage of phone surveys is that you can clarify questions for the respondents, which you cannot do in an e-mail or mail survey. Phone surveys are also attractive because the data can be compiled instantly into a database.
    * **In-person surveys** collect a lot of information from each respondent and allow you to clarify questions. You can also show respondents a product and see their facial expressions. While these surveys can take more time and money (hiring interviewers)

to execute, I have conducted hundreds at festivals and events. Sometimes it's just easier to reach people when they are all in one place: Have clipboard, will travel.

5. **Focus groups.** A focus group brings eight to 12 participants together in a sort of "board room" environment with a large table and comfortable chairs, to see a product, taste test it, talk about it—whatever your objectives are. You can observe the group members' behavior, and you can ask them questions similar to those you might place on a survey. Focus group participants talk for an hour or so about what the product/service means to them and why they bought it (or if they would buy it). A good group can provide a lot of information through discussions, but sometimes one or two people dominate those discussions.

To prevent this, use a moderator to lead the discussion. To get the most out of your focus group, you should prepare a discussion guide of the topics you want to cover, and use it to stay on point. It is also important to pay respondents—usually $100 to $200 for an hour-long meeting—so they are motivated to attend the session. Videotaping the meeting will give you a record of the discussion, but you still have to compile what everyone said into a transcript and pull useful information out of it. Making sense out of all those comments can be fairly time-consuming.

DESIGNING A SURVEY

Designing a survey is not hard. We've all taken surveys, so we all know how they're put together. Making sure the survey is designed the way you want it is imperative, though, because once it goes out the door, you can't change it, for the most part.

First, **determine your objectives** for the survey. Start by writing down all of your ideas, and then **choose the top three objectives**. If you have more than that, you might want to do multiple surveys at different times. As you choose, ask yourself if you want to know:

* Who your customers are: their ages, genders, ethnicity and household income, for example
* If they are satisfied with your product/service
* How they found out about your firm and why they decided to buy from you

These are just a few examples. The point of narrowing down your objectives is to keep the survey brief. It can be tempting to add just a few more questions, and then a few more, and then just a couple more. All of a sudden, your survey is non-functional because people either won't take it or won't finish it. We'll discuss the importance of this again in the next section.

Second, now that you have determined the general themes for the survey, **write the questions**. You can ask a question like, "How did you hear about us?" Or, you can get the answer through a declarative statement like, "Please indicate your overall satisfaction on a scale from 1=Poor to 6=Excellent." Each question or statement should measure only one concept.

Professional marketers avoid "double-barreled" questions, like, "Was the airport friendly and safe?" A high score on a dual question like that will not reveal whether the participant thinks the airport is friendly or safe or both.

Third, **choose an answer style for each question**. For instance, you can start the survey with simple yes/no questions to ease people into the exercise and get them thinking about the topic. Then you can add more difficult questions, including "rating" questions, which ask people to rate their satisfaction or agreement on a numerical scale. These answer styles are known as **quantitative or closed-ended questions**. Respondents like them because they offer a framework for the answers. They're also relatively easy for you to interpret: A rating of 5 is better than a rating of 4, for example. Some examples of closed-ended questions are:

* **Rating questions.** Use even scales—4, 6, 8 or 10 response options. Although psychologists advocate the use of odd scales—3, 5, 7, 9— because humans are comforted by a neutral point (on a five-point

scale, for example, a score of 3 would be neutral), marketers don't want people to have a neutral option. We want them to choose "one side of the fence or the other"—so on a six-point scale, a score of 3 is negative, but 4 is positive, for example.

Also, balance your scales. A scale that ranges from 1=Good to 6=Great is biased because it omits any kind of negative ratings. While no one wants to be rated poorly, not giving that answer as an option affects the integrity of the survey data.

* **Ranking scales** ask people to order a set of items based on their preferences; that is, only one thing can be ranked No. 1; one can be No. 2, and so on. Ranking scales take the respondent more time to complete than a yes/no or rating scale because they have to make decisions. A ranking scale forces the respondent to place weights or importance on different items; with a rating scale, they can rate every item the same. With ranking scales, you can determine what the respondents value most. Still, ask them to rank no more than six items.

It's always a good idea to include some **qualitative or open-ended questions** on a survey so that respondents can tell you in their own words why they rated your firm a certain way or how they think you can improve your service, for example. The answers to qualitative questions can provide rich detail, but you have to figure out a way to code or categorize all of the open-ended responses that you get. Is there a general theme? Are the comments generally positive or negative, or split?

So limit the number of open-ended questions you ask. Otherwise, respondents will grow tired of having to write or type in their answers, and the answers will take you too long to analyze.

Fourth, **clean up the survey with uniform formatting and by proofreading**. Add a welcome statement that explains the survey's purpose, when the respondent needs to complete it, what the incentive is for completing it, an assurance that the responses will remain confidential, and a thank-you for participating. A survey littered with spelling, grammar and punctuation mistakes signals that your company is not detail-oriented or professional.

Fifth, **write instructions that are very, very clear.** Indicate if participants should "Check All that Apply" or "Check Your Top Reason" or "Continue on the Next Page." When in doubt, over-explain as most of the participants are in a hurry to finish the survey.

Finally, **test your survey.** Give it to co-workers, friends and family members, and time how long it takes them to finish it. Even if they know little about your industry or firm, they can still offer feedback on questions and instructions that are unclear.

THE RIGHT SAMPLE SIZE?

An important goal of any survey should be a good response rate. Improve yours by:

* **Following the KISS method: Keep It Short, Stupid.** Your survey should take a respondent three to five minutes to complete. Worry more about time than about the number of questions.
* **Giving a deadline and an incentive for meeting it.** You can offer each person a coupon, keychain or another small token of appreciation or have a drawing for one or two decent prizes, like a free product or service from your company or a gift card. The drawing creates less work for you, and even if it's for something inexpensive like a $25 Starbucks gift card, it can dramatically increase response rates.
* **Update your mailing list.** Before you mail or e-mail a survey to your past customers, update your database of addresses or you will wind up with few responses and a lot of bounced e-mails.
* **Buy a screened list from a reputable list broker.** This isn't cheap, but buying a list from InfoUSA or Experian, for example, can increase the response rate. For instance, if you own a rare coin shop and want to know what potential customers think about collecting coins, you will get a better response rate by paying a few thousand dollars for a

list of people who have an interest in rare coins than by sending your survey to random people.
* **Remember that you are collecting a *sample*.** You're not conducting a census. A census aims to measure everybody; you probably can get the information you need by surveying a limited number of people.
* **Enlarge your sample.** The bigger the sample, the better your results will be. In rare cases, a sample that's too large can have an adverse impact on the statistical properties of a survey, but small-business owners don't need to worry about this.
* **Don't worry if your sample is small.** Believe it or not, 30 completed surveys is a statistically valid sample. Of course, this is the bare minimum for a sample size, and it won't be enough if you want to compare sub-groups like male vs. female respondents.

HOW TO USE THE RESULTS

Once you collect your data, put it to work for your business. Tucking it away in a drawer is a waste of your time and money.

Perhaps the results of the research seem overwhelming, but they don't have to be. If the survey is designed right on the front end, the analysis will be easy.

Organizing the data into basic pie charts and bar charts can help your data tell a story in the simplest way. Use your data to come up with three to five strategic recommendations that will help your firm. Some might be actions you can implement fairly easily, while the others might be more long-term. Regardless, you'll be able to back up all five with your marketing research, so the data—and not just your opinion—is justifying your recommendations.

Finally, take action. If you survey your customers or employees on how you can improve your business, and then do nothing with the research, it can upset those employees or customers who took the time to respond. If you survey your employees about their compensation and benefits packages, but don't make any changes based on their responses, for example, it can appear you never intended to change anything. Why ask the questions if you don't want the answers?

Marketing research really doesn't have to be difficult. With a well-thought-out plan to collect and use information, you can add significant value to your marketing and sales strategies.

THE MARKETING AND SALES LINK

Salespeople are often referred to as "boundary spanners"; that is, they work outside of the walls (boundaries) of the firm, and in many cases, visit other firms (if they are in business-to-business sales) or even people's homes. They see your products/services being used by the consumers, and they interact with them. So why not get salespeople involved in the survey design process? They can help you ask the "right" questions.

DO YOU BARK?

Brainstorm:
* If you had to create a lab experiment for your product/service, what would it entail? What variables would you manipulate?

Assess:
* Find a survey from another firm and critique it. What are the things that you like about the survey and the things that you would change?

Rank
* What is the top area about which your firm needs to survey its customers?

Keys to Implement:

<u>Attack Dog Key to Defend Your Turf</u>:
Hold one focus group with current customers within the next three months.

<u>Attack Dog Key to Hunt Your Prey</u>:
Mystery shop at one of your competitors this month.

CHAPTER 4
THE SNIFF TEST

What does your firm's strategy look (smell) like?

JEB'S GEMS
    *   Finding Your Niche
SCOTT'S STEPS
    *   SWOT Analysis
    *   The Product Life Cycle
    *   Perceptual Mapping
THE MARKETING AND SALES LINK
DO YOU BARK?

> *"Would you tell me, please, which way I ought to go from here?"*
> *"That depends a good deal on where you want to get to," said the Cat.*
> *"I don't much care where," said Alice.*
> *"Then it doesn't matter which way you go," said the Cat.*
>
> —From *Alice's Adventures in Wonderland* by Lewis Carroll

JEB'S GEMS
FINDING YOUR NICHE

If a parent at an after-school soccer match were to ask you what your small business sells, could you answer in three sentences or fewer?

Could you give a really *good* answer? One that would persuade her to consider hiring you?

Companies that sell one thing, like windows or bicycles, have it easy. Their answers are quick and simple.

But remodelers and builders don't sell a single thing. In fact, we don't really sell "a thing" at all. We sell our services. Sometimes, that's hard to explain.

Still, when you have a chance to promote your business, even to one potential customer in the bleachers of a grade-school soccer match, you need to do a thorough job.

In one to three sentences.

Even if you do sell windows, you need to have the right pitch to convince someone to buy your windows instead of another company's. Are your windows vinyl, wood, aluminum, or all of those? Do you install windows, finance them, custom-size them? If you sold bicycles, your one- to three-sentence pitch would reveal whether you repair bicycles, as well as sell them, and if you buy used bikes, too.

Later in this chapter, Scott talks in-depth about evaluating the strengths and weaknesses of your company's products and services, so you'll have your best chance at selling them. He'll talk about "positioning" your product or service in a way that shows consumers that yours is *different* and *better* than anyone else's.

Before you can do any of that, you have to know exactly what your product or service is. And you have to be able to squeeze everything your "public" needs to know about it into one to three sentences.

Some people call this an "elevator speech," and lots of small-business owners say they don't need one.

You need one.

It gets back to your unique business proposition and your mission statement. Knowing how to succinctly describe the best thing about your product or service keeps you focused. It keeps your employees focused. It focuses your customers. It gets everybody going in the same direction.

Let's use JEB Design/Build as an example. Without any prompting, my employees might have told that soccer mom that the firm designs and executes remodeling projects. That's true enough.

But as the business owner, I want them to be more thorough and specific when that mom, or any other client or potential customer, asks what the company is all about. So they're trained to say the firm does upper-end remodeling for clients who want a full-service approach that includes design. They say our best customers are homeowners who have had a bad prior experience with another contractor and are looking for a good experience. They say JEB Design/Build won the Angie's List Super Service Award.

Three sentences. They get potential customers in the door.

Part of a successful marketing effort is to get everyone in the company focused. Every employee should know the company's niche, what its ideal customer looks like and how important it is to me that we earn top ratings on customer service surveys.

As you'll learn later in this chapter, evaluating your product or service's strengths and weaknesses is an important step in marketing that product. Here's another good idea that I always pitch to the remodelers and builders who have asked me to help them beef up their sales and marketing efforts: Make a list of what you *don't* want for your company, as well as what you do want. It's an instructive exercise that will help you really focus on a niche.

Nobody at JEB Design/Build, for instance, wants to build dog houses, or decks, unless they're custom decks and are part of a larger project. Our firm turns away homeowners who need a single door installed, and we don't take on commercial or industrial projects. I'm willing to take on the right high-end custom homebuilding project, but I'm not at all interested in building tract houses or subdivisions.

The result: We work on custom kitchens and bathrooms, whole-home renovations and room additions, among other major projects.

Don't make yourself a jack of all trades. Your success will come from your niche. Your niche is your brand. Think about yourself, your product and your company as that brand.

Look at McDonald's. That's a hamburger restaurant. You can get a salad there, but it's always going to be known as a burger place. Burgers are its niche.

Specializing in your niche product will give customers and potential customers something to "know" you by. Choosing your niche and sticking to it makes your product or service easier to market. If all you do is kitchen makeovers, for instance, that's all you have to advertise. And your niche makes it easier for you to make money. If you specialize, it's easier to turn a profit because you get really good and highly efficient at that one thing you do.

SCOTT'S STEPS
SWOT ANALYSIS

Understanding your environment is critical for any business owner or manager, and for all of the employees, for that matter. If you don't know where you are, how can you know where you want to go?

So conducting a **situational** or **environmental assessment** is one of the first things you need to do when you are developing your marketing strategy. One of the easiest ways to do that is via a **SWOT** analysis.

The goal of the SWOT analysis is to give you a good understanding of your Strengths, Weaknesses, Opportunities and Threats. To start the analysis, you'll make a list of these.

Strengths and weaknesses are "internal" to your company; that is, they are things you can control to some extent. But opportunities and threats are "external" to the firm because they affect the industry as a whole.

Your **strengths**, of course, are the things that your firm does really well. Maybe you've been in business for a number of years, have an experienced management staff, high brand awareness, special technology and equipment, strong capitalization or even a patent or a trademark. All of these things give you an advantage.

On the other hand, **weaknesses** are potential areas that make you vulnerable. Maybe you are new to the industry, have lost some experienced employees or have a relatively unknown brand name.

Be very honest with yourself as you list your strengths and weaknesses. You can try to ignore your weaknesses and fail to address them, but your competitors will not. You might think you have a really strong brand identity, but what do others think?

So get input from employees, customers and vendors in order to create a balanced, 360-degree perspective of your firm.

The **opportunities** are the variables that your firm—or any firm in your industry—could capitalize on over time. Conversely, the **threats** are the things that could negatively affect your firm—or any firm in the industry. Some areas can be either an opportunity or threat, like economic, social, technological, legal, political and competitive forces. Let's take a look at some of them.

The economy, of course, affects almost every business. But some industries are more recession-proof than others. And some industries, like pawn shops and Laundromats, benefit from a downturn in the economy. Social trends can also affect an industry for better or worse. For instance, some companies that have embraced the green movement have benefited, for the most part, over the last 10 years or so. Similarly, technology can have a dramatic impact on an industry as we've seen with the Internet since the 1990's.

Also, many industries are affected by changes in the legal and political system that can present either opportunities or threats. Industries such as healthcare, education, pharmaceutical and military/defense need to continually monitor the latest legal trends.

Finally, there is the competition. You need to look at both your current competitors *and* your future competitors, and at the barriers to entering the market. You might not have much competition today, but that could change overnight. Also, keep in mind that substitute products and services can take away your sales.

Let's look at some examples of companies that failed to examine their environments. In 2001, Imperial Sugar, a leading producer of refined sugar with very few domestic competitors, had to declare bankruptcy. Why? The firm's leaders had failed to predict the growing use of artificial sweeteners, such as Sweet'N Low, NutraSweet, Equal, Splenda and many others. While Imperial Sugar survived by improving its operational efficiency, it definitely learned a valuable lesson. Similarly, in the 1990's, Penn, makers of tennis racquets and tennis balls, was struggling. Fewer and fewer people were playing tennis and sales were flat. To someone's credit, the firm did a thorough SWOT analysis and discovered a significant opportunity: While people weren't playing tennis, they might still buy tennis balls—at PetSmart—for their dogs. They rebranded the same product at triple the price (anything for Skip!), and it saved the firm.

While it is such a simple concept, many small-business owners don't think they have the time to research and evaluate their internal (strengths and weaknesses) and external (opportunities and threats) environments. However, it doesn't take that much time, and every firm should do it at least once a year—and more frequently in turbulent industries. Without a SWOT, you might as well be driving with a blindfold.

THE PRODUCT LIFE CYCLE

Every product and service goes through four stages in its "lifetime." The first stage is often referred to as the **Introductory** stage. Here, a new product or service is launched into the marketplace. Firms spend time and money to make consumers aware of this new offering. Profits are low at first because sales are slow when people are unfamiliar with the product or service and the company is spending a lot of money on research, development and advertising.

Once the product or service gains some traction with consumer purchases, however, it enters the **Growth** stage. At this point, sales really start to take off. With success comes competition, and many new entrants crowd the space. Then, over time, many of the competitors have come and gone and the product enters the **Maturity** stage.

Lastly, the product or service enters the **Decline** stage. While the product or service in decline is still available in stores and online, the company usually just rides it out without devoting time and money to marketing it.

The VCR player is a great example. It had a long run as the dominant household media device for more than 20 years. When it was first introduced, consumers weren't really sure how it worked or if it was worth the price; some of the first VCRs cost almost $1,000 in 1980, and they had early competition from the

Sony Betamax and laser disc players. Once the VCR player gained acceptance, many electronics firms jumped in to make their VCR brands, and sales soared. Over time, the market matured and eventually declined when the DVD player, a superior device, was introduced. The DVD player had many advantages over the VCR. It had digital video/audio, more easily jumped to different parts of a movie without fast forwarding or rewinding a tape, had disks with more storage capacity for extras and outtakes, and the disks were touted as more durable than tape. Additionally, the DVD player was not completely foreign to consumers. It used the same coax cables as the VCR and worked like the CD-ROM on our personal computers. Altogether, it made for a much better product. Today, streaming movies are quickly pushing the Blu-ray or any other movie playing device into decline.

Tied to the product life cycle is the **diffusion curve**. This is the rate at which a product spreads or diffuses throughout the population. The people who like to try new things and are willing to pay more for new products when they first come out are usually the high-income, highly educated **innovators,** who make up a very small percent of the population. Next to buy are the **early adopters** and then the **early and late majorities**, and finally, the **laggards**—usually lower income, lower education and older consumers who may never adopt a new product.

The important thing is to recognize where your product or service is in the product life cycle, and how many people have adopted it, so you can adjust your marketing strategy accordingly.

The product lifecycle is for product and service categories, not individual brands. However, the creators of some brands have looked at where their products or services are in their life cycles and have come up with innovative ways to extend the life of the brand. One example is Arm & Hammer Baking Soda, which was originally created for use in baking. Yet as boxed cake mixes captured the market, fewer people baked from scratch, so fewer people used baking soda. So Arm & Hammer began marketing its product as a refrigerator deodorizer, which was successful. Then, when this product was about to enter the decline stage again, Arm & Hammer scanned its environment and entered the carpet deodorizer, laundry detergent, deodorant and other product categories in the 1990's. In recent years, Arm & Hammer has again started marketing its product as a refrigerator deodorizer, some 30 years after that first campaign, because marketers there believe that is alive again.

Who knows? We may see Arm & Hammer come full circle to once again market baking soda for baking. Overall, the product's history is a good example of marketers who know where their product is in its lifecycle, and then adjusting it to survive.

PERCEPTUAL MAPPING

In marketing, we often talk about how a brand is positioned. **Positioning** is how you want your customers and potential customers to "see" your brand in relation to your competition. This goes back to our Chapter 1 discussion about "how different you are," or your differential advantage.

An easy way to visualize this concept is via a **perceptual map**, which is a graphical display of your positioning. Often, it is a simple two-dimensional graph with an X and Y axis. While the axis dimensions are up to you, it is usually best to use price as one of the axes.

Years ago, I did a consulting project for a for-profit crime lab. While the lab's prices were about the same as the city and county crime labs, its turnaround times on DNA, blood splatter, ballistics and other tests was far superior. I created a perceptual map to show their differentiation. The result: Smaller suburban cities purchased this small lab's services instead of building their own labs or using a major city's lab.

The perceptual map shows different points for the firm: **desired positioning** and **actual positioning**. The desired point is where you aspire to be, and the actual point is where you currently reside, based on employee feedback, customer surveys, market analyses and other research. By listing both, employees can visualize where the business owner wants the firm to be, and then they can help it get there.

In their book, *Blue Ocean Strategy*, W. Chan Kim and Renee Mauborgne implore business owners to find an area of the market with many customers, but few competitors. Using the analogy of sharks, the authors claim that red oceans are very competitive markets, where numerous "sharks" (firms) fight over bits and pieces of market share. Blue oceans, on the other hand, are markets with an unmet customer need, but few, if any, firms.

The best example the authors offer is of the company that created the theatrical circus production Cirque du Soleil. The Canadian founders of the firm loved the circus and wanted to start a new one. Yet, the expense of running a circus is very high, with all of the animals, their feed, transportation and handlers. The founders also knew that consumers took their whole families to the circus and didn't want to pay a lot for tickets.

So they created a blue ocean: a circus-like show with the acrobats (but no animals) and added music so that they could charge Broadway prices, escaping the price elasticity of the regular Barnum & Bailey circus. The result: a multi-billion dollar business with shows all over the world.

Of course, as we discussed throughout this chapter, you have to be able to adapt to changes in the market. **Re-positioning** your brand is doing just that. You aim to alter consumers' perceptions (on the perceptual map). You can do this by creating a totally new product or brand, which can be very expensive. Or you can try to convince people that your current product or brand is more luxurious, less expensive or otherwise better.

In other words, you are trying to rebrand your current offering and let people know that the "new and improved" you is better on some dimension.

Pabst Blue Ribbon did a great job of this a few years ago. The brand went from a budget beer for the working man to a trendy budget beer for the young, alternative/indie rock set. Notice that the company changed its brand identity, even as it kept the price low.

A more drastic re-positioning occurred with Abercrombie & Fitch. Most people don't realize that it was originally a high-end hunting and fishing outfitter for older males, including President Teddy Roosevelt. Then, A&F rebranded to become a teenage, casual clothing brand with controversial and often risqué marketing campaigns.

Together, these three tools—SWOT, product life cycle and perceptual map—will let you know where you are and help you get to where you want to be.

THE MARKETING AND SALES LINK

A SWOT Analysis is a great tool for a firm to use. It's also a great tool for a salesperson. Specifically, salespeople should be prepared to address any of the firm's weaknesses. As mentioned earlier in the chapter, companies that casually dismiss or fail to acknowledge their weaknesses will have a problem. If you are not honest with yourself, your competitors will not be as nice and will be sure to point out your weaknesses. So make a list before you meet with a client and have an explanation or plan of action to address each one.

DO YOU BARK?

Brainstorm:
* When do you think your product/service category will go into the decline stage of the product life cycle? Is there a way to prevent your product/service from entering the decline stage?

Assess:
* Create a perceptual map for your firm. Label the X and Y axis with the two most important variables and mark your firm ("actual" and "desired" positions) and competitors on the map.

Rank
* What is your firm's biggest strength? Biggest weakness?

Keys to Implement:

<u>Attack Dog Key to Defend Your Turf</u>:
Eliminate one weakness within the next year.

<u>Attack Dog Key to Hunt Your Prey</u>:
Outline one new opportunity every quarter.

CHAPTER 5
THE TAIL WAGGING THE DOG

Getting employees excited about the brand

JEB'S GEMS
   * What's Your Brand?
SCOTT'S STEPS
   * The Link Between Brand Identity, Brand Loyalty and Brand Equity
   * What's Your Brand's Personality?
   * To Extend (the Brand) or Not to Extend?
   * Managing the Brand
THE MARKETING AND SALES LINK
DO YOU BARK?

> *"An orange ... is an orange ... is an orange. Unless, of course, that orange happens to be a Sunkist, a name 80 percent of consumers know and trust."*
>
> —RUSSELL L. HANLIN,
> PRESIDENT EMERITUS, SUNKIST GROWERS, INC.

JEB'S GEMS
WHAT'S YOUR BRAND?

I used to wear a suit and tie whenever I would meet with any homeowner who had hired me for a remodeling job or was thinking about it. Before long, everyone around Shreveport was calling me "the gentleman builder."

I knew another remodeler who wore a cowboy hat and boots every day, and people pegged him as a cowboy builder, even though he wasn't a cowboy, and he never referred to himself as one.

The fact is, whether you have identified your company's "brand," whether you advertise it or whether you have never even thought about it, you have one.

Your brand is what people know about you. If you're just starting out in business, your brand is that you're new to the game. If the sign on your company van is simple, people will think you're a no-frills person, and that's part of your brand.

Whatever cues you give people will become your brand.

If you're just starting out, a big cue is the way you dress. If you wear nice shoes or work boots, jeans or dress slacks, a shirt with a logo or a T-shirt with holes in it, people will notice that and identify you with it. It doesn't matter if it's what you intend or not. You're creating a brand for yourself.

Be aware of those cues. If you're trying to attract high-income customers, a removable, no-frills truck sign might not send the kind of cue that will get them on board. You might have to paint or "wrap" your logo on your truck instead.

Even your choice of a van or a truck sends a message to would-be customers: In the remodeling industry, for example, a van appears "service-oriented," like a plumber, while a truck looks like it's for someone who works in construction.

Don't unintentionally create a brand for yourself. Do it on purpose. Take charge of it.

I didn't mind it that people called me a "gentleman." But I wanted JEB Design/Build to be known as "the remodeling team you can trust." And now, because I put that language out there on every piece of literature, on every one of my vans and on every ad I buy, that's how my company is known.

Of course, a small business can't create and build a brand through advertising alone. Small-business branding is about what people think of you, your employees and the work you do. So do it as if your reputation depends on it.

It does.

If you go to my Web site, *www.JEB.net*, you can download and use my "Cafeteria Approach to Branding" to help you define what your brand is.

Here's where I advise the remodeler and builder clients of my consulting practice to start: Decide what you want people to think of when they hear your company's name.

When you hear "McDonald's," you think "burgers, fast, cheap, convenient." "Federal Express" means "fast, overnight mail, easy, professional uniforms, lots of stations, expensive."

What do your customers think of when they hear the name of your competitor's company? They should think of something different—something better—when they hear yours.

When homeowners are deciding between two contractors, they pick up on what they've seen and heard of you. They use those cues to evaluate you. You want those cues—that brand—to say to the customer: "I like that. That's for me."

Not every consumer is going to say, "That's for me," and that's OK. Your brand should attract the kinds of clients that you want: People who value the kind of service you offer, and are willing and able to pay the price you charge.

SCOTT'S STEPS
THE LINK BETWEEN BRAND IDENTITY, BRAND LOYALTY AND BRAND EQUITY

Branding has become a popular buzzword in the business press the last 10 years. Yet brands have been around much longer than that. Winemakers in ancient Greece would offer their "brand" in a uniquely shaped or colored glass bottle so that their wine stood apart from others at the market. Similarly, cattle ranchers in the 1800's here in the U.S. started to label their livestock with a fiery hot piece of iron: a brand. That way, people could identify cattle by their mark—or brand—and know the ranch.

Today, nearly every product or service is branded. Even in categories that we traditionally think of as commodities, we see strong brands such as Sunkist, Dole, Starbucks and Kleenex. And we now see companies from all over the world working to develop their brands. In 2006, I took a class of MBA students to meet with executives in China. In one visit to China's Department of Commerce, an assistant director told us, "If you can make it, we can fake it," alluding to the high number of counterfeit products sold in the local markets. Returning with a different class of MBA students in 2010, a Chinese executive told us, "Chinese firms are really investing in their brands in an effort to differentiate themselves from low-quality products made in other Asian countries."

So China gets it now.

A number of things work to form your brand. While we often just think of the brand name, logo and slogan, there are other variables. For instance, the age of your firm (Google is seen as young and trendy), industry (all brands in fitness apparel might be perceived as "athletic"), country of origin (Italy is known for fashion), the owner's or CEO's image (Lee Iacocca and Chrysler were closely linked at one time), advertising style (Absolut's artistic print ads) and celebrity spokesperson (Flo with Progressive Insurance) can affect your brand's image. Even your product's or service's attributes can shape consumer perceptions of your brand.

Let's look at some examples from a favorite product category: beer. While many beers look and taste the same, breweries have done a great job of giving their brands unique identities. A beer light in color? It must have fewer calories. An imported beer? It must be sophisticated. Add in advertising, sports and entertainment sponsorships, and endorsements, and each brand is able to attract a loyal following.

Why is branding important? If you can create a brand with a strong image or identity, consumers will become loyal to your brand. And with brand loyalty comes brand equity. But let's back up for a minute.

What do these terms mean? **Brand identity** means consumers have heard of you—or your product—and know something about what you do and have positive feelings about your brand. Once consumers develop an affinity for your brand, you hope that they become **brand loyal**. That is, your consumers consciously and consistently buy from you—and sometimes they are willing to pay more because they know what to expect from you. In turn, you can charge a higher price. This premium means that your brand has equity.

While often debated among accountants, **brand equity** is an asset that can be placed on your balance sheet—albeit an intangible asset. Of course, there are some low-price providers, such as Walmart, that still have a large amount of brand equity because their customers are very loyal to them because they know what to expect: consistently low prices.

Coca-Cola has one of the highest brand equities in the world according to consulting agency Interbrand. That's right. A company that makes carbonated sugar water has a brand equity in the billions. What this means is that if Coke were to sell its brand today, it would be valued at much more than its physical assets, like inventory, factories and equipment. That is, there is value in the Coke name, logo, slogan and other attributes associated with it.

So as you can see, there are many reasons to try to increase your brand's equity. Once again, brand image leads to brand loyalty, which leads to brand equity.

WHAT'S YOUR BRAND'S PERSONALITY?

Let's take a look in more detail at your brand's identity. About 20 years ago, Stanford Professor Jennifer Aaker studied the **personalities of brands** in detail.

Personalities? Yes.

She concluded that consumers do see brands with human characteristics, such as **competence** (*The Wall Street Journal*), **excitement** (Disney), **sincerity** (Hallmark), **ruggedness** (Marlboro) and **sophistication** (Rolex). Since her seminal work, a number of other researchers have confirmed her findings and extended them to many different categories, countries and purchase situations. So believe it or not, consumers do see brands as having some human traits.

Of course, that shouldn't be a surprise. Dartmouth College Professor Kevin Lane Keller and others have advocated for years that the brands we purchase are an extension of ourselves. While consumers may indicate that they buy a product or service because it is the cheapest or most convenient, for example, the brand personality plays a big part, as well.

TO EXTEND (THE BRAND) OR NOT TO EXTEND?

Another decision that owners and managers need to make with regard to their brands is whether and when to extend the brand. As we've discussed, you want your brand to have value (or equity). When it does, you might be able to leverage that equity by creating new brands or co-brands.

When you create a new brand in a different product or service category, yet use your original brand name, you create a **brand extension**. This could be very successful for your firm. Your customers already indentify with your brand. So by assumption, they will purchase your new brand, too. If so, that's great. If not, it can be a problem.

In fact, sometimes, a failed brand extension can erode the original brand equity that took you years to build. The key is that you want to extend your brand into categories that consumers can believe. For example, Hooters restaurants have extended into wing sauces and seasonings. Do consumers believe that Hooters can make these products? Sure. But, what about Hooters Air? Would you trust Hooters to operate an airline? Apparently not. That was an actual, but failed, brand extension that lasted only three years.

Similarly, a business owner or manager may decide to align a company's brand with a brand from another firm. Through this synergistic approach, both brands can benefit. This was the case when Lexus and Coach (interior leather) teamed up in the mid 1990's and dramatically increased sales. However, like a failed brand extension, a bad **co-branding** agreement can be catastrophic. Moreover, co-branding can be more risky because you don't run your partner's company.

MANAGING THE BRAND

David Aaker, Professor Emeritus of Marketing at University of California Berkeley, has often insisted that managers treat their brands like the captain of a large ship. The captain is continually monitoring the vessel to make sure it is in good shape, and if he wants the ship to make a turn in two miles, he needs to start thinking about it now. In other words, the captain can't turn the cargo tanker at the last minute—or turn it back the other way right after that. These large ships are just not that agile.

While you want your company and employees to be responsive to fluctuations in the market or unexpected order changes, you need to look at the brand from a long-term perspective. Changing components like the name, logo or slogan of the brand overnight will lead to consumer confusion. If your logo is red and blue one month, red and black the next and red and yellow the next, you are hurting your brand identity. Consumers won't know if you are the same firm with which they are familiar. Unfortunately, this example is no exaggeration; it happens more often than you'd think.

Of course, you can make changes to your brand, but they need to be well thought out, subtle, and maintain the consistency and integrity of your established brand identity. Having said that, someone needs to be officially in charge of the brand. If two or more people are tinkering with the logo or using different slogans, it hurts the brand image. You need just one Brand Captain in order to maintain your brand identity, loyalty and equity that have taken you years to develop.

THE MARKETING AND SALES LINK

People buy brands—not just any product or service. As a salesperson, you are selling your brand. Let's define "your brand" for a minute. There's the brand you work for (i.e., your firm's brand), the brand your firm sells, if you are a distributor/retailer, and your own personal brand. As they are to products and services, customers are loyal to a salesperson because they identify with him or her. As such, the firm, product and salesperson brands all need to be somewhat aligned. The salesperson who works at a Chevy dealership but drives a

Ford is not good for either's brand identity. While salespeople don't have to own the brands that they sell (in some cases they really should), they definitely shouldn't be bashing them, either.

DO YOU BARK?

Brainstorm
* If you had to pick a firm to create a co-branded product/service, which one would it be?

Assess:
* Does your brand image have a consistent look and feel (on your trucks, employee uniforms, letterhead, advertising, etc.)?

Rank:
* Which of the five brand personality facets (i.e., competence, sincerity, excitement, sophistication and ruggedness) best describes your brand? Name only one.

Keys to Implement:

<u>Attack Dog Key to Defend Your Turf</u>:
Create a brand decision tree within the next three months.
(i.e., Who can make what changes to the brand?)

<u>Attack Dog Key to Hunt Your Prey</u>:
Within the next month, pick 10 customers who are loyal to your brand and ask them to refer your firm to five other people.

CHAPTER 6
BARKING UP THE WRONG TREE

Are you targeting the right customers?

JEB'S GEMS
 * Listen Twice as Much as You Talk

SCOTT'S STEPS
 * Micro- vs. Macro-Marketing
 * How Consumers Make Decisions
 * Target Markets: Going Beyond Demographics
 * Selling to Other Businesses

THE MARKETING AND SALES LINK

DO YOU BARK?

> *"Behavior is a mirror in which everyone displays his own image."*
>
> —JOHANN WOLFGANG VON GOETHE
> GERMAN WRITER

JEB'S GEMS
LISTEN TWICE AS MUCH AS YOU TALK

The wise Greek philosopher Epictetus said, "We have two ears and one mouth so we may listen more and talk the less."

That guy could have sold ice to an Eskimo.

Ask any customer why she decided to work with you instead of with one of your competitors. Somewhere in the answer you'll hear, "They didn't listen to me."

Small-business owners are problem solvers. They know how to plug a leaky roof, how to calculate a bigger tax refund or how to talk a client's way out of a speeding ticket. They're proud of their technical knowledge, and they figure if they regale a customer with how much they know, they'll get the sale.

Wrong.

Telling your customers how smart you are isn't going to sell them. Asking them to tell you about their needs and dreams is.

Ask, don't tell.

And *listen* when they tell you. Jot down their requests and descriptions. Ask follow-up questions so they'll tell you even more. Take it all in, and remember it.

You know how to solve a lot of problems, for sure. But you can't solve any customer's problem until you know what that customer *perceives* her problem to be.

For the client with a leaky roof, that leak might not be the biggest problem. She might be reluctant to hire you—a stranger—because she got ripped off last week by an unscrupulous contractor who took off with her down payment and never repaired the leak. Her problem is that she doesn't feel she can trust another roofer—no matter how many of them she interviews.

You're not going to know that if all you're doing is talking about what a great patch job you're going do on her roof.

Save that for later. For now, just let her tell you about it.

When she's finished, tell her stories—true stories. Tell her about your other client who was also betrayed by another roofer, and explain that you agreed to wait for payment until after you fixed her roof. Let her know that when you hire contractors to work at your own house, you always ask for a signed contract detailing the scope of the job, how much it will cost and when payment is due—and offer her such a contract. Give her examples of clients whom you have worked with again and again over the years because you and they have developed a mutual respect and trust—and give their phone numbers to her so she can check you out.

Set yourself apart by listening. This client doesn't need to know you're smart; she probably figures that's a given. She needs to know she can trust you.

Customers very often let their emotions dictate which company to hire. So reach for those emotional reasons. Trust is a huge emotional issue for a homeowner. And trust starts with listening.

Even if the client starts the conversation by telling you which color shingle she prefers, bore in beyond the "bricks and sticks" until you get to the emotions behind the job. Yes, she needs some new shingles. But no, she's not going to hire you unless you assure her that she can trust you.

Any roofer can patch up a hole. Let the client know that you're the unique one who understands that her peace of mind is more important than properly stopping the leak.

If you and your employees really listen to your clients and make them feel that they're truly being "heard," you will be among the rare small businesses that do that. Your ability and willingness to listen—and not your skills—will be the thing that sets you apart from your competitors.

Listen and learn. Listen and understand. Listen and make the sale.

SCOTT'S STEPS
MICRO- VS. MACRO-MARKETING

In its prime, the iconic TV show *I Love Lucy* drew some of the highest Nielsen ratings ever. While it was a good show, it would never draw ratings that high today.

Why? With hundreds of channels, consumers now have many choices, and a lot of them are ditching their TVs altogether to watch their favorite shows and movies online.

So the days of **macro-marketing** are long gone. With macro-marketing, a firm would place an ad on a popular show on one of the "big three" TV networks

(Fox wasn't around yet in those days) and hope its product or service would interest some of the people watching. Many marketers used to call this a "shotgun" approach.

Micro-marketing, on the other hand, targets a very specific group of people—usually a smaller group of people. Unlike the shotgun approach, micro-marketing uses the "sniper" approach: one consumer at a time, with precision. Even if you think your product or service is so great that everyone should buy it, you need to determine who is the *most* likely to purchase it.

If you have an existing business, the easiest way to do this is to try to find customers like your current ones. I worked for a number of years for a hospital system in Fort Worth, Texas, with 10 primary care clinics. When we studied the basic demographics of our clinics' patients, we determined that 70 percent of one of our physician's patients were women; 60 percent of another's were families; and 80 percent of a third doctor's patients were African-American. Using direct mail, billboards and other means, we tried to attract similar types of patients to each clinic.

Another example: Several years ago, the owners of a new gym wanted to meet with me to show me their marketing plan. They wanted to target single males, ages 25 to 35. Their marketing plan revealed the reason: They wanted to be the "Hooters of fitness centers," with a scantily clad, all-female staff. So they knew exactly the kind of customer they wanted to attract to their business. Or did they?

Elsewhere in the plan, the owners had devised strategies to attract single females and families with children. They figured it wouldn't hurt to try to attract other kinds of members besides young men. In fact, I told them, it *could* hurt them.

They needed to decide what their target market was—and own it. If it's young, single males, then it's young single males. By trying to hedge their bets and market to everyone, they could end up alienating all of the groups.

HOW CONSUMERS MAKE DECISIONS

Chapter 1 explained that marketers rely on psychological concepts to better understand why people buy the things they do. Let's take a quick look at the steps or stages that we, as consumers, go through when we purchase a product or service.

> Stage 1: **Problem Recognition.** If your car stereo quits working, you have a problem. It's not the end of the world, but the difference between the *intended state*—I want to hear music—and the *actual state*—nothing is coming out of the speakers—results in a problem.
>
> Stage 2: **The Search.** This stage includes two levels: the internal search and the external search. During the **internal search**, you think about your experiences with the product, and you search your long-term memory to form a **consideration set** that narrows down the brands of car stereo you would consider buying. During the **external search**, you consult sources other than yourself, like *Consumer Reports*, a retail salesperson or your friends, for information on the product category.
>
> Stage 3: **Evaluate the Alternatives.** Here, you compare the prices, quality and features of the various brands you are considering.
>
> Stage 4: **Purchase.** You decide on one brand and buy it.
>
> Stage 5: **Post Purchase.** This is when you evaluate whether you made the right decision. At this stage, as marketers, we want to minimize what's called **cognitive dissonance** or **buyer's remorse**. That is, we want people to feel good about their purchase and often provide warranties or customer support hotlines, for example. If people regret buying your product—even if it's excellent—it's not good for your firm.

Consumers go through all of these steps, regardless of what they are buying. In some cases, they go through them very quickly, and may not even realize they're doing anything. Psychologists call this **involvement.** A high-involvement product is something that takes more time, energy and processing because it's relevant and important to you. Homes, vacations and cars are usually high-involvement products and services, which means the consumer spends more time at each of the five stages.

On the other hand, with low-involvement products like potato chips, you go through the same five stages very quickly.

TARGET MARKETS: GOING BEYOND DEMOGRAPHICS

Most companies **segment** the marketplace—that is, they split it into groups of similar people—as part of their marketing effort. The five primary kinds of segmentation are:

Demographic. Using U.S. Census or consumer survey data, you can focus your marketing effort on consumers in a certain age group, or by gender, ethnicity or income. For example, Fiesta Mart supermarkets target Hispanics. Centrum Silver targets older consumers. Lady Foot Locker targets women. Tiffany & Co. and BMW target high-income consumers, and many businesses target low-income individuals with offers of car title loans and furniture rentals, for example. **Family life cycle** is also an important part of demographics. Two couples with the exact same household income may have very different purchasing habits. A couple with young children may spend money on daycare, swimming lessons and minivans, while an "empty nester" couple goes on Alaskan cruises and supports the arts, now that their children are grown and out of the house.

Geographic. Some organizations target people in specific countries, regions, states, cities or ZIP codes. For example, some manufacturers of pick-up trucks target Texans and create specific ads just for that state. Even more specifically, you can do **geodemographic** segmentation, right down to a particular neighborhood or city block. Marketers often say, "You are where you live." In other words, everyone in a specific neighborhood probably is somewhat similar: As a group, they might have an average of 2.2 children and drive certain brands of cars. Marketers often rely on data from Nielsen, whose PRIZM segmentation system classifies every household in the country into one of 66 segments such as Blueblood Estates, White Picket Fences and Shotguns & Pickups, as examples.

Psychographic. This form of segmentation tells marketers what makes you "tick" as a person. Through surveys, marketers learn about your activities, interests and opinions: if you like to ride motorcycles on the weekend, collect stamps or think schools should teach religion, for example. A company called

Strategic Business Insights created a psychographic survey called the VALS and has administered it to thousands of customers. You can take the survey yourself at *www.strategicbusinessinsights.com/vals*.

Benefit. Often, consumers look for different benefits when buying a car. One buyer might want good gas mileage, while others may value towing capacity, and some others seek luxury. Car companies know this, so they target consumers based on the benefits they seek. **Benefit segmentation** might seem like "splitting hairs," but keep in mind that benefits are different from product attributes. An attribute, for example, is high horsepower or torque. A benefit of high horsepower or torque is that you can tow your boat or camper. While you can market both attributes and benefits to consumers, remember that consumers think in terms of benefits.

Usage. A catalog company keeps a running list of what each of its customers has bought all year. At the end of the year, it might rank its customers from "who spent the most" to "who spent the least." The next year, it will target the top 20 percent of spenders because it believes in the **Pareto Principle**, which says the top 20 percent of customers buys 80 percent of the merchandise the company sells. As it targets this group, though, the company doesn't forget everybody else. But its main focus is on the top 20 percent.

Using these micro-targeting principles, you can learn as much as possible about your current and future customers. Whether you collect the information yourself, hire a research agency or buy the data, it will be well worth the investment. To just assume that you know your customers—and forgo the hard numbers—is a marketing mistake.

SELLING TO OTHER BUSINESSES

Before a business makes a purchase, the decision-makers go through the same five stages that the individual consumer does. Still, purchase decisions in a business are more formal and time consuming, and often involve committees, limits on spending authority and input from multiple people.

Price, however, generally is not as important to businesses that are buying products and services as it is to consumers. Instead, firms prefer reliability, the relationship with the other business and flexibility when dealing with their vendors.

For example, a hospital purchasing agent, of course, wants to get the best price on surgical supplies. But the hospital needs more supplies to arrive every day. If the supplies don't show up, the hospital might have to cancel surgeries, and that could lead to huge losses of revenue. So for the hospital, the dependability of the vendor is even more important than the price, and it is willing to pay more for that dependability.

Your firm, like most, probably buys its supplies three different ways:

The **straight re-buy** is an automatic kind of re-order, a sort of "automatic pilot purchasing" for office supplies and other materials you routinely use. It takes very little effort.

The **new buy** involves products your company has never bought before, so you'll look at the items in detail and do some comparison shopping by sending out a request for proposals. You'll also evaluate the vendors.

The **modified re-buy** is the marketing term for products that you might have bought before, but you want to bid the purchase out anyway to learn about new, similar products, vendors new to the market and changing prices.

When you sell your products and services to other businesses, be aware of the type of "buy" your customer is making. Too many sales reps assume that everything from their existing clients is a straight re-buy, and then they're blindsided when their customer says, "We've decided to solicit bids from other companies."

When selling to a business, you'll also need to know who is in your customer's **buying center**. The buying center is *more* than just the purchasing department. Look at your own company. Are there people throughout the organization who have a role in buying products, but do not necessarily work in the purchasing department?

Let's look at these roles with examples from the hospital I worked at for a number of years:

Gatekeeper. An administrative assistant usually plays this important role. Someone who is rude to the gatekeeper is unlikely to get past the gate.

Users. The users of surgical blades in a hospital are the surgeons. They're not even employees of the hospital, but as users, they have a lot of influence with the buying center.

Influencer. Likewise, the operating room director wants to make the surgeons happy, so he or she might try to influence the purchasing decision. Other influencers might be in the Total Quality Management (TQM) Department or on a committee that evaluates products.

Decider. This might be an individual or a team whose members vote on product purchases. At our hospital, the CEO and vice presidents met each Wednesday to vote on major purchases.

Purchaser. This is probably a purchasing agent or a director of materials management, who issues the purchase order, negotiates freight and signs off on the purchase.

It is important to determine each person's role and level of involvement in the process. Also, know the politics of the buying center at your customer's business. It might seem that marketing and selling directly to surgeons makes sense, in my example, but it could upset the others with a role to play in the purchase.

Just as you can segment consumer markets, you can also segment the business-to-business marketplace. One way to do this is to use **North American Industrial Classification System (NAICS) codes.** Each industry and industry subset is assigned a unique code, and then it is further classified based on what it does. Using these codes, you can "drill down" into an industry.

For instance, NAICS code 23 includes all firms in construction. A more specific code, 236, is construction of buildings. Still more specific, code 236118 identifies only those firms in residential remodeling and you can search by country, state or ZIP code.

Using NAICS codes and other information, you can micro-market when you sell to other businesses, just as you can when you sell to consumers.

As we've examined in this chapter, you *can't* (as we say in the South) just market to everyone. You have to have an understanding of how your customers (business-to-consumer or business-to-business) make purchasing decisions and know something about your customers, like their demographics, usage or psychographics.

THE MARKETING AND SALES LINK

To be the most efficient salesperson, you'll want to see the most potential clients in the least amount of time. Running down leads that end up in a "dead end" can be very frustrating. In Chapter 9, we'll talk about using Integrated

Marketing Communication (or IMC), which includes advertising, public relations and direct mail, among other methods to reach potential customers, and how an effective IMC strategy should generate sales leads. Yet, qualifying these leads is equally important. When you **qualify** a lead, you are making sure the prospective customer is seriously interested in purchasing your product or service. Does the customer have the financial means to buy the product or service? Is he or she interested in purchasing relatively soon? Qualifying, though, does take some subtlety. I've heard numerous stories of sales personnel at car dealerships asking to run your credit before they even show you a car. Yes, that is qualifying, but it's also rude. So have your customers tell you about themselves and their purchasing decision process (*be sure to listen*) to help you determine if they are the right customers for you.

DO YOU BARK?

Brainstorm:
* List the best way that your firm can minimize or subdue a buyer's remorse.

Assessment:
* What VALS type are you? Do you agree with this assessment? What VALS type(s) are your customers?

Rank:
* What's the No. 1 way you can become a better listener?

Keys to Implement:

<u>Attack Dog Key to Defend Your Turf</u>:
Develop a full profile (demographics, psychographics, usage, etc.) of your current customers within the next three months.

<u>Attack Dog Key to Hunt Your Prey</u>:
Buy a list of potential customers who fit that profile within the next six months.

CHAPTER 7
THROW ME A BONE

Going above and beyond to exceed customer expectations

JEB'S GEMS
    *   Surveys Improve Service
SCOTT'S STEPS
      *   Customer Satisfaction Made Simple: The Gap Model
      *   How do you RATE(R)?
      *   Lessons from Top Service Providers
      *   Why You Need to Match Your Supply with Your Demand
      *   It All Starts with Your People
THE MARKETING AND SALES LINK
DO YOU BARK?

> *"We see our customers as invited guests to a party, and we are the hosts. It's our job to make the customer experience a little bit better."*
>
> —JEFF BEZOS
> CEO OF AMAZON.COM

JEB'S GEMS
SURVEYS IMPROVE SERVICE

My friend Ty Melton likes to tell a story about the cable TV technician who came to his Colorado home five or so years ago to hook up his TVs. The guy seemed like he'd rather be anywhere else but at work, barely spoke to Ty and performed the task so poorly that Ty, a design/build contractor like me, had to call the cable company and request that a different tech come out and finish the job.

A few years later, when Ty moved, the cable company sent the same tech to his new house. But this time, that same guy wanted to know exactly what Ty needed, made sure everything worked before he left the house and treated Ty like the most important customer he'd ever had. On his way out the door, he mentioned that the cable company would be sending Ty a survey so he could evaluate the tech's work.

What a difference a survey makes.

Between the time of their first meeting and their second, Ty's cable company had started asking every customer to fill out a customer service survey after every job. One result: The employees stepped up their customer service efforts so clients would not write anything negative on those surveys.

You might have noticed the last time you bought or rented a car or had one serviced. The big players in the automotive industry—from Honda to GEICO to Enterprise—are tying performance reviews, and sometimes bonus money, to the results of customer service surveys, and their employers are going out of their way to make sure their clients give them high marks.

Your employees will do that, too, if you make those survey results count when it comes to raises, bonuses and promotions.

Better customer service is just one of the ways surveys can benefit even a small contracting company. At JEB Design/Build, we rely on our surveys—conducted by a third-party survey company called GuildQuality—to let us know:

* **How satisfied our customers are with us.** Our results teeter at around 91 percent, and our goal is 100 percent. The most important question on the survey: How likely are you to recommend us to someone else? Our goal is that every client will be willing to recommend us.

* **If a client has any lingering complaints**. Because we get survey results back quickly, we can immediately resolve any unfinished business a customer has with us. For some reason, some clients don't tell us face-to-face when they're unhappy. Learning it while we can still do something about it is far better than hearing later that a homeowner bad-mouthed us to potential clients or wrote a negative review about us online.
* **What we need to change**. Surveys can reveal trends. If more than one client says the subs left dirty footprints on the carpet, for instance, I know I need to insist that they cover their work boots with fabric "booties" before they walk on anyone else's carpet. If customers complain about foul language or stray sandwich wrappers or smoking in the house, I know how to put a stop to that, too.
* **What management might not otherwise know**. Customers who fill out surveys aren't shy about reporting on the behavior of your crews—good and bad. An owner or manager can use this information to teach, discipline, praise or promote.
* **What customers like**. Beyond uncovering customer complaints, surveys are a forum for your clients to sing your praises. We like to share those positive comments with our customers in the form of testimonials on our Web site.

Start surveying your clients, and you could see customer service—and satisfaction—improve almost immediately.

SCOTT'S STEPS
CUSTOMER SATISFACTION MADE SIMPLE: THE GAP MODEL

Today, the majority of America's Gross Domestic Product (GDP) is in service industries. While we often talk about bringing manufacturing back to the U.S., the fact is that the U.S. is a service economy. Thus, delivering a high level of customer service is critical—even for those who produce products.

Why? Because consumers can compare product attributes—they can "kick the tires" so to speak—companies have to provide some added value to the finished product in order to differentiate themselves from everyone else who sells the same thing. This might include customer support centers, warranties, on-time delivery or financing options, for example.

Very, very few organizations don't have to worry about customer service. Sure, some government agencies don't seem to care about it. But, it will eventually catch up to them. Just ask the U.S. Postal Service, which has seen its market share erode as FedEx, UPS and other competitors gained traction over the last 30 years.

Think about your own experience as a customer. You know when you are happy or not with a service encounter. But do you know why? The fact is that our satisfaction is based on our expectations. In other words, if the level of service that you receive is above what you expected, there is a positive "**gap**," which means you are satisfied: The service provider exceeded your expectations. On the other hand, if the service you receive is below what you expected, there's a negative "gap," and you are dissatisfied: The provider didn't even meet your expectations.

Customer satisfaction is related to expectations. We expect a higher level of service if we go to an expensive, five-star steakhouse, for example, than when we eat at a fast-food restaurant.

HOW DO YOU RATE(R)?

In the 1980's, marketing researchers at Texas A&M University, including Valerie Zeithaml, Leonard Berry and A. "Parsu" Parasuraman, discovered that regardless of industry, consumers look at a service provider's **Responsiveness, Assurance, Tangibles, Empathy** and **Reliability**—RATER—when evaluating any service they receive.

Responsiveness means we want service firms to promptly answer our calls or seat us, for example.

Assurance means we want service employees who have the knowledge and skill to help us.

Tangibles are things like the décor and cleanliness of the service provider. Even though by definition, services are intangible, consumers look for tangible cues such as sights, sounds and smells to see what kind of service to expect. These are part of the **servicescape** or **atmospherics** of a firm.

Empathy means we want the employees of a business we deal with to put themselves in our shoes if there is a problem with, for example, service delivery.

Reliability means we want some consistency in the service we are paying for, even though some variability is inevitable in any service produced by people (versus machines). If we go to a restaurant one night and have a great experience, go back the next week and have a sub-par experience, and then go again the following week and have a decent experience, we might abandon the restaurant altogether. We don't want a "roller coaster" of service.

LESSONS FROM TOP SERVICE PROVIDERS

Each facet of the RATER model can be addressed through employee **training**, **empowerment** and **service guarantees**. Every firm puts employees through some kind of training. But, Walt Disney World has really been a leader in training its employees to "follow the customer service script."

A long time ago, Disney World executives recognized that people go there to escape reality and have fun in the theme park's fantasy land. Disney also knew that a family of four spends a lot of money there in a week, and that it only took one "grumpy" employee—pun intended—to ruin a family's "escape."

So Disney adopted a number of specific policies and procedures that all employees are to strictly follow. Some examples: Employees are referred to as "cast members," and once they emerge from the below-ground employee dressing room and step into the park, they are "on stage." Employees are expected to take their jobs seriously, smile, and be groomed and dressed appropriately at all times. Also, to help employees see the "big picture," Disney requires employees to rotate through a number of jobs at the park.

The result: Disney wows its customers. The process works so well, in fact, that the Disney Institute trains executives from many different industries all over the world on how to do the same thing.

While training, policies and procedures are critical, giving your employees the freedom to handle a customer service issue is equally vital. At Ritz-Carlton hotels and resorts, front-line employees are **empowered**.

Management experts agree that it's difficult to give people responsibility without also giving them some kind of authority. Recognizing this, Ritz employees "own" customer complaints. That is, if a hotel guest stops an employee in the hall with an issue, it is up to that employee to resolve it. The employee can't say, "I'm just a housekeeper. You'll have to call the front desk."

So if you are ever a guest at a Ritz-Carlton hotel, you won't experience what Arizona State University researchers call "ping-ponging"—when you call a service provider with an issue and get transferred from department to department.

To help them solve problems, Ritz gives every employee several thousand dollars to spend on resolutions. If a guest says he suspects a housekeeper broke his sunglasses while cleaning his room, the employee he complains to has 30 minutes to log the complaint, determine the options—like buying the guest a new pair of glasses or giving the guest some cash, for example—and report back to the guest.

"Sure," you may be thinking, "Ritz-Carlton can do that. It's a premium luxury hotel." But the practice, like most things, is scalable. You may not be able to give your employees several thousand dollars to spend on resolving customer issues, but could you give them $100? Or $10?

Most companies don't because they're afraid employees will abuse the system and "give away the farm." But, like Ritz-Carlton, you can audit the petty cash account to make sure all customer issues are legitimate and that employees can account for the money.

Companies that give their employees the financial power to help customers often report that their employees usually err on the side of the company, giving away less merchandise, services and money than a manager would have.

While employee training and empowerment are important, so is making sure your customers know what to expect when they visit your company. That's why more and more companies are creating platforms to show that they stand behind their work.

JetBlue Airlines, for example, has a Customer Bill of Rights that clearly outlines what the company will do in case of a service failure. It says, in part, "Customers who experience an Onboard Ground Delay on Arrival for 1-1:59 hours after scheduled arrival time are entitled to a $50 Credit good for future travel on JetBlue" (Retrieved from http://www.jetblue.com/p/about/ourcompany/promise/Bill_Of_Rights.pdf).

A lot of companies will never offer an explicit **service guarantee** or **customer bill of rights** for fear that they will lose a lot of money if something goes wrong. The fact is that if you make a mistake, you're probably going to lose a lot of money anyway in the form of lost customers, via word of mouth (Go to YouTube and check out how many people have viewed "United Breaks Guitars" to see what can happen when a customer service issue goes viral)—unless, of course, you make it right, which marketers call **service recovery**.

So you might as well put it out there for all to see. When you do that, you let customers know you are serious about customer service and you send that same message to your employees.

That said, if you do offer a guarantee, it needs to be specific—to protect the business—yet easy to redeem if a failure occurs—so the process doesn't further irritate the customer.

WHY YOU NEED TO MATCH YOUR SUPPLY WITH YOUR DEMAND

Evaluating supply and demand information may seem like something academics and economists need to worry about. But, as a small-business owner or manager in services, you too, need to have a handle on this.

It's important to match your supply with your demand, as best as you can. If you are overstaffed, just in case of high demand, you waste resources when employees just stand around with nothing to do if things turn out to be slow. Conversely, if you are understaffed for the demand, then the level of customer service may suffer.

The solution is to try to predict or forecast the demand so you can be prepared.

The first thing to do is look at your historical sales data. Are sales higher during different times of the year? Do sales vary during the week or even during hours in a day? What other variables could be affecting demand?

Take, for example, a professional baseball team. Several years ago, the Atlanta Braves began to develop forecasting models for attendance. Of course, the season occurs primarily during the summer and more people attend weekend than weekday games. But, they were also able to pinpoint increases in attendance when school was out for the summer and for games against certain opponents. The result: They were able to dramatically improve their attendance predictions.

Other teams have created their own models and added other attendance boosters: the team's win-loss record; nice weather; promotions like discounted tickets, post-game concerts and bobble-head giveaways; and a lack of competing sports or entertainment events in the area.

If done properly, **demand forecasting** can make your business that much more efficient and make your customers more satisfied.

IT ALL STARTS WITH YOUR PEOPLE

One of the reasons why many businesses have lost their way on customer service is technology.

Gaining popularity in the 1990's, Customer Relationship Management (CRM) systems became the talk of business. With an investment in mainframe servers and software, you could capture all of your consumers' information and make customer service as easy as a keystroke. Today, as customers, we wind our way through a maze of phone menu items, obediently entering our customer ID number over and over, and then finally, when we make our way to a human representative, we're asked again, "Can I get your customer ID number?"

Where's the progress? Technology cannot take care of customer service for you. Good customer service requires people.

At the end of the day, customer service is not that complex. Companies make it more difficult by putting so many barriers in place. They create policies and procedures that are strictly geared toward improving operational efficiency, not customer service. They don't reward or punish employees based on customer service. They invest in computer systems, thinking they will replace the human touch. Wrong, wrong, wrong.

Design your service from the customer's point of view. It's not that tough. In fact, when in doubt, think of customer service as if you are hosting a party for friends and family at your house, as Amazon CEO Jeff Bezos suggests in the opening quote of this chapter: You clean your house. You buy enough food and drinks. You greet your guests at the door and take their coats. You make them comfortable. You continually offer them more food and drinks throughout the party. You make sure they're happy.

Shouldn't your business do the same for its customers?

Humans are social creatures. We live in groups, work in groups and interact in groups. For the most part, we like being around other people. So why not get the best people you can to work for your company: people who like being around others and helping them?

Done right, customer service can be a differentiator for a firm, like it is for USAA, L.L. Bean and Trader Joe's.

But, it doesn't happen by accident. It takes a plan. In 1975, singer David Allen Coe and songwriter Steve Goodman thought they had the perfect country and western song with "You Never Even Called Me by My Name." They then realized that to have the perfect song in that genre, you needed a formula. You had to say something about mama and trains and trucks and prison and getting drunk. When you did, it would result in a top hit, which it was.

Customer service is the same way. Create a simple recipe and make employees practice it, and it will work (Yes, former NBA All-Star, Allen Iverson, we are talking about "practice." You can go to YouTube to see his infamous press conference).

THE MARKETING AND SALES LINK

The era of relationship marketing is here to stay. That is, every firm is better served if it develops a long-term relationship with its customers. When a business does that, it's much more efficient than to continually look for new customers. The problem is that many salespeople still practice the "snake oil" sales approach of the Wild West. In those days, the salesman went from town to town, claiming to sell a new elixir that would make people younger. But, they *never* went back to a previous town for fear that the customers there may be a little disgruntled.

While the adrenaline rush of making a new sale can be infectious, you don't want to forget about your past customers. They are your lifeblood.

Several years ago, prominent Dallas car dealer Carl Sewell convinced his salespeople to look at the lifetime value of each customer. Once he showed the sales team that every customer was potentially worth several hundred thousand dollars, sales increased—and so did customer service. Check it out in his book, *Customers for Life*.

DO YOU BARK?

Brainstorm:
* Which company's customer service impresses you? How could you incorporate something that it does in your business?

Assess:
* Look around your firm and take a picture of the best-looking area (atmospherics, servicescape, décor-wise). Now, take a picture of the worst area.

Rank:
* If you could create only *one* customer service policy, what would it be?

Keys to Implement:

<u>Attack Dog Key to Defend Your Turf</u>:
Implement some form of job rotation within the next three months.

<u>Attack Dog Key to Hunt Your Prey</u>:
Publish a Customer Bill of Rights this year.

CHAPTER 8
THE LEAD DOG

Creating a culture of teamwork by leading by example

JEB'S GEMS
   *   Training: It's Not for Everyone
SCOTT'S STEPS
   *   Leading vs. Managing
   *   There is a T (for Trust) in Team: Working Together
   *   Recruiting, Selecting, Training and Retaining Team Members
   *   "Firing" Bad Customers to Maintain Team Morale
   *   Seeing the Big Picture as a Team
THE MARKETING AND SALES LINK
DO YOU BARK?

> *"Leadership is the art of getting someone else to do something you want done because he wants to do it."*
>
> —DWIGHT D. EISENHOWER
> 34TH PRESIDENT OF THE UNITED STATES
> AND FIVE-STAR ARMY GENERAL

JEB'S GEMS
TRAINING: IT'S NOT FOR EVERYONE

When an employee excels and exceeds your expectations, the next logical step is to get that superstar into a training program that will turn him or her into a leader and onto a career path with your company.

In my experience, that doesn't always work out.

I hired a bright, customer-oriented sales rep, trained her, mentored her and coached her until we both realized that she simply wasn't any good at selling, mostly because she really didn't like doing it. So we had to part company.

I did everything I could for her, and I believe she tried her best. It just didn't work out because sales simply wasn't for her.

You can spend gobs of time and money on training employees to be better sales reps, to manage the departments where they're doing such a good job, and to take on greater responsibilities that will put their talents to even better use. But if an employee isn't into it, you're wasting your time and money.

Nobody can dispute the value of orienting new employees so they understand how you do things at your company. That can take days or weeks or even months, depending on the nature of the job. And few would argue that huddling with employees every day or at least every week to keep everybody up-to-date on changes and new rules—and for a pep talk and a reminder about the firm's values and customer service policies—is a great idea.

But pushing existing employees—no matter how promising they seem—into courses, seminars, certification programs or training classes won't turn them into leaders if they don't want to be leaders. "Teaching" someone how to be a good sales rep won't turn that employee into a good sales rep if he or she doesn't have any talent for selling.

Not everybody wants to be trained. Not everybody wants to be promoted. Not everybody who works for you intends to make a career at your company.

There's really nothing wrong with that unless you make it a problem by forcing the employee into something he or she just doesn't want to do. That's an employee who's going to be looking for another job in short order.

Not every employee is at a place in life where he or she can embrace the opportunity you're offering. Some don't want to work as hard as they would have to if they were promoted. Others might be OK with working in a lower-level job that allows them to leave on time every single day and to truly "leave the office behind" at quitting time so they can give their full after-work attention to their families.

I had that experience with a draftsman who was talented and ambitious, and he wanted to grow, expand, get promoted and move into the leadership ranks—after his kids grew up. During the time he worked for me, though, it wasn't the right time in his life for his career to take off.

That was OK with me. I knew I couldn't force him into a job that he didn't want.

My point—and it's one I constantly make with the remodelers and builders who take advantage of my sales and marketing consulting services: Small-business owners need to spend their training dollars carefully.

My advice to them and to you: Don't waste your training budget on people who don't want the training. Don't go broke trying to "change" an employee who just wants to put in her eight hours and considers the job "just a job."

How can you know which ones are "into" it? I ask my employees, in a nonthreatening way, if they want training and if they're interested in taking their careers to the next level. We talk about their career goals. And I make training available to employees, so it's there if and when they want it.

Sure, you need to have ongoing staff and department meetings, and you can use part of every meeting to keep everyone's skills and attitudes fresh. You can also spend a few minutes during those meetings reminding employees that training is available to anyone who wants it.

But don't force them into it. Put the onus on the employee to seek out training, to choose to take the training and to let you know once they have it and are ready to put it to use for your company.

Employee training can't be one-size-fits-all, either. Different kinds of training will be relevant to different employees, depending on their jobs, the jobs to which they aspire and their life circumstances.

Unless a particular job requires ongoing renewals of certifications, it's unlikely that you'll get your money's worth from requiring employees to participate in training.

One bookkeeper at JEB Design/Build took all of the required training, and she did a great job. I wanted to retain this excellent employee, but she was looking around for something bigger and better. I threw ideas and training opportunities at her, offered her a promotion and tried to turn her into a manager.

What she really wanted was to become a CPA. So I helped her pay for the courses she needed. And then she quit and went to work for a CPA firm.

As managers and owners, we think we are a great influence in our employees' lives, but for most, this is just a job. They're going to do what they're going to do. She wanted to be a CPA. There was no job for a CPA at JEB Design/Build.

Other employees, though, can take a little training and really take off. They're ready and willing. Make sure the training is available to them when they're ready.

Suppose you were a gardener. You'd make sure the ground is tilled and the soil is full of nutrients before you put a new plant in the ground. You'd water the seedling, ward off bugs, build a deer fence and maybe tie the plant to a stake to help it grow.

After that, the plant sort of has to take it from there, right?

Even the best leader can't "make" any employee bloom and grow.

What you can do is require a certain level of performance and make the training available to those who feel they need it to meet that requirement. And another thing you can do is dismiss employees who do not perform to that level, despite your efforts.

Here's what I tell those remodelers and builders who come to me for coaching and advice about their businesses: Make your requirements perfectly clear to every employee—and make the consequences of not meeting those requirements clear, as well. Give your employees the tools they need to meet those requirements.

Some will embrace those tools and grow like weeds. Those are the ones who are worth the money you're willing to spend to train and retain them.

SCOTT'S STEPS
LEADING VS. MANAGING

Everybody thinks he or she is a leader. Ok, not everyone. But, a lot of people profess to be leaders, including many of today's younger generation. Who wouldn't want to be a leader? It sounds like a great job. You just tell people what to do, and then you get all the credit.

Not so much. There's a lot more to being a leader than telling people what to do.

Let's begin our discussion by distinguishing between leading and managing.

Managing involves four major duties: planning, organizing, doing and control.

- **Planning** is determining what needs to be done and communicating this to others.
- **Organizing** is figuring out who is going to do what by when.
- **Doing** is taking action to complete the plan.
- **Control** occurs when the manager assesses if the plan worked. If not, changes or adjustments to the plan can be made.

Leadership is different from management in the sense that it is more long-term, strategic and innovative, as it involves thinking of new ways to improve your organization's product or service. However, the biggest difference, as President Dwight D. Eisenhower noted in the opening quote of this chapter, is that although a lot of people can manage, few can truly inspire others.

Not every quarterback with a strong arm is a leader, for example. The great ones seem to lift up their whole team and rally their teammates to play as hard as they can. They're the leaders.

It's the same in business. Not everyone is a Steve Jobs. Yet, as a small-business owner, you can still inspire all of your employees to market or sell your brand. The key: Believe in the brand yourself.

So many small-business owners eventually say their businesses have worn them out. That's no surprise. It takes every ounce of energy to start a business, work seven-day weeks, deal with the stress of losses, and continually prove themselves to their customers. However, if the small-business owner can weather the hard times and bounce back with enthusiasm, the staff will, too. It will be contagious.

Unlike a Fortune 500 firm, where some employees don't even recognize their CEO (The TV show, *Undercover Boss*, proved that.), employees of a small business watch the owner very closely. Leverage that: Be excited and proud to market and sell your brand, and your employees will be, too.

THERE IS A T (FOR TRUST) IN TEAM: WORKING TOGETHER

HP co-founder David Packard once said, "Marketing is too important to be left to the Marketing Department." He could not have been more right, especially for a small business.

Marketing takes a team effort. Professors in MBA programs assign team projects, requiring groups of four to six students to work together to complete a task. Students often bemoan the team project because working with others takes coordination, tolerance of others' ideas and compromise.

That's precisely why professors assign team projects.

In today's business world, you have to be able to work with other people. In fact, many executives complain that one of their biggest organizational challenges is getting employees to work together on teams. This is especially true for cross-functional teams with employees who report to different supervisors, but are assigned to work together on a common project.

Still, teamwork creates "synergy" among its members, whose combined, total effort is greater than the individual effort of each teammate.

What makes for a good team? Here are some keys:

* R-E-S-P-E-C-T.
* A little less talk and a lot more action.
* If you ain't first, you're last.
* Happy cows make great cheese.

Just like the classic Aretha Franklin song, you have to make respect for your teammates the top priority. That doesn't mean you have to agree with your team, but you can at least politely debate the issues. I've worked with hundreds of teams. They spend too much time talking. At some point, the team has to take action, as Elvis once crooned. And if people don't ask for tasks, assign them. People on teams often want to proudly pontificate about the issues, but they become real quiet when it's time to volunteer to do the work. Too many times, teams just try to plow through and simply finish the project. But, why not strive to excel and "win the race" every time as Ricky Bobby's father preached in the movie *Talladega Nights*. Lastly, have fun. You get to work on a project with other people instead of having to do it all by yourself. Just like the happy cows in the ad campaign for California cheese, if you're having fun, you will produce better results.

Seems like common sense, right? Still, student and employee teams seem to suffer more meltdowns than the guests on a Jerry Springer episode. The teamwork usually begins with a friendly exchange of ideas. Yet, as the deadline draws closer, tempers flare and the claws come out, and team members argue, betray and manipulate each other. It would make a great reality TV series.

It doesn't have to be that way.

A team, whose members trust each other, doesn't engage in that kind of drama. In their insightful book, *Who Will Do What by When,* authors Tom Hanson and Birgit Zacher Hanson assert that trust is a critical ingredient in getting a team to perform. As a member of a team, you want your teammates to trust you, and you need to trust them.

A big barrier to trust: If you say you will do something by a certain time and then don't, how can your team members trust you? To them, your gaffe appears selfish.

The old adage, "There is no 'I' in team," is so true.

RECRUITING, SELECTING, TRAINING AND RETAINING TEAM MEMBERS

In a small business, every hire is critical. Your marketing success depends on your good employees.

It is the job of *everyone* in the company to market the company. It's a team effort. So do everything you can to strengthen your team. Here are the foundations:

Recruiting. Retailers often complain about the people who work for them. But they're the ones who hired them. You can't excuse your employees' poor behavior by telling your customers that you can only afford to pay minimum wage or that the talent pool in today's market is weak. Instead, use your new marketing skills to market your company to high-quality potential employees. Some keys for recruiting good staff:

* **Pay well.** Keep in mind that if you pay more than minimum wage, you can expect more from your employees in return. That strategy is working for The Container Store, which pays about double the average of the retail industry. In turn, the employer expects triple the work.
* **Create realistic job descriptions.** When you post a help-wanted ad, make it realistic. You'll be more likely to attract applicants who have skills, experience and personalities that will fit your company's culture if you advertise for what you really want.

If you're recruiting employees to work for a company that's involved with concerts, for example, you could recruit people who love music—and you'll get tons of applications. But you'll waste your time weeding out the ones who are not willing to work nights and weekends, or travel, or stand on their feet for 12 hours a day. You need team members who are willing to work hard. Say so in your job postings so that candidates know this before they apply.

Selection. It takes due diligence to hire the right employees. Learning about an employee's qualifications, checking references, conducting background checks and interviewing are critical. Digging deep enough to learn whether a job applicant enjoys problem-solving and working with customers will help you identify the right people for the job you're offering. Don't make the mistake of hiring too quickly or of hiring just anybody to fill a slot.

Training. Like Disney, your company needs to teach new employees your rules and expectations. You also need to teach them a skill I call Customer Recognition Management. As your employees develop relationships with your customers, they need to realize that each one is different: Some want to chat every time they come into your shop. Others just want to buy their products and get in and out. Front-line employees need to learn to recognize what each one wants.

An example: A restaurant manager I know trains his waiters to focus on "glasses and eyeballs." They constantly scan their tables so they can keep iced tea and water glasses full at all times and notice it the second a customer looks up from his or her meal in search of the waiter.

Waiters there have to keep their heads up—and never stare at the ground as they walk out of the kitchen. Noticing a customer's body language and temperament, the manager told employees, is the first step to delivering great customer service.

Putting employees through a new-hire orientation or one-time training is not enough. Specific, relevant and periodic training are the keys to keeping customer service at the top of their minds. The training can be as informal as a five-minute team huddle at the start of the day. But the key word is "relevant," as we noted at the beginning of this chapter.

Ritz-Carlton, for example, asks employees to learn and follow a handful of key concepts for superior service. Managers focus on a different concept in a quick meeting each day. Training on these concepts is specific. For example, employees are frequently reminded to answer the phone within three rings.

Retention. Hiring excellent employees who "get it" when it comes to marketing service and customer service isn't the end of the hiring process. You have to work hard to keep the good ones.

One simple retention tool is recognition. While everyone appreciates a pay raise, that's not the only thing you can give your employees to keep them happy. Also effective is a mention in the company newsletter or a salute during a team meeting. Other alternatives to more money: Offer your best employees more autonomy, more influence in management decisions or a flexible work schedule.

When you do hand out raises, don't give them across the board. Not all employees perform equally well, so not all deserve the same pay raise. Rewarding everyone with the same amount is akin to punishing those who excel at their jobs. You need to pay those who deliver the highest level of customer service more than those who aren't as interested in keeping your clients happy.

Indeed, as we discussed in Chapter 7, some firms are tying pay increases and bonuses to customer satisfaction scores. Others are even taking "internal customer service" into account when it's time for raises, and paying more to team players. Combined, the practice creates a true merit pay system, based on customer service.

"FIRING" BAD CUSTOMERS TO MAINTAIN TEAM MORALE

The customer is always right. Right?

Maybe not.

Customer satisfaction is so critical that we have identified retaining your customers as the No. 1 job of the Attack Dog Marketer. Yet every company has some customers who are just a pain in the you-know-what.

These difficult customers complain about even the smallest things, and they do it often. They continually ask for free "extras." They return products with little or no explanation. And in some cases, they belittle or insult your employees. In the end, you spend an inordinate amount of your time making this small sample of customers happy—and you might even wish they weren't your customers at all.

Fire them.

Be nice about it; offer to help them find another firm to meet their needs.

Or simply raise the price they pay for your service so it reflects the extra time and trouble they're causing you. Refuse their requests for "extras." Or just politely tell them that they need to find another company.

You will immediately feel freer and less stressed-out, and you can redirect the energy they once required to your other clients who appreciate you and tell others how great you are. A bonus: Your employees will feel the same sense of relief and renewed energy. Nothing builds team morale like getting rid of a negative energy source.

SEEING THE BIG PICTURE AS A TEAM

Customer service is important at the individual level. But employees also need to see the "big picture" of your organization's customer service effort.

Here are three tools that will help your employees understand the big picture:

Service blueprint. Also called a **customer contact diagram**, a service blueprint is a visual display of every step the customer takes. For instance, someone who flies with an airline purchases a ticket, goes to the airport, parks a car—if applicable, gets a boarding pass, checks luggage, walks through security, waits at the gate, boards the plane, flies, lands and gets their luggage at baggage claim. At each of these **contact points**, the customer interacts with an airline employee or computerized ticket kiosk. At each contact point, the company has the opportunity to either delight or disappoint that customer.

So having everyone on your employee team "walk in the shoes" of the customer will reveal to the staff how the customer experiences this process. Have employees create a pencil-and-paper diagram of the process and identify where it could be improved.

Don't leave out the employees and processes from the "back of the house" that customers never see. Even they contribute to the customer's experience and often are the answer to a service breakdown.

You can do this exercise for any kind of business. Just keep in mind that your customers don't care what goes on behind the scenes. They want their hamburgers cooked their way in a timely fashion. Problems in the kitchen aren't the customer's concern. Fix them without excuses.

Give your employees the experience of being your customers. Once they walk in those shoes, they will give better service.

Job rotation. Every employee should also experience working other jobs in the firm's other departments. This further enables them to see the "big picture" of customer service and how the work of all the departments and jobs fit together. As we've seen, Disney is a big believer in job rotation. Similarly, parcel company UPS has a long history of requiring new employees to start out working the loading docks.

Despite the benefits, though, very few companies have any kind of job rotation, probably because it takes some coordination and planning. Plus, some managers believe if an employee from one department is working in another department, it will hurt the productivity of both departments. That could be true, but the short-term loss in productivity will be offset in increased productivity, better teamwork and enhanced customer service in the long-term.

Plus, job rotation doesn't have to be a formal program. You could simply assign employees to spend a few hours a month in different departments, shadowing various personnel, especially if the employees do not have the proper training to work in certain areas. By simply observing, an employee can learn and perhaps even provide a fresh perspective on how to improve things in that department. At the very least, the "shadow" employees will get to know more of their colleagues.

Internal customers. Both employers and employees too often consider the people who purchase their products and services—their external customers—as their only important customers. Whether you're the boss or a co-worker, treating your internal customers—the employees—with the same respect and courtesy as you treat your paying customers is important to customer service. One reason: It's not easy to turn your "niceness" on and off. In other words, after screaming at a fellow employee in the back office, it's difficult to walk into the showroom and politely greet a customer. The way you treat your employees or co-workers will "bleed over" into the way you treat your customers.

Similarly, keep your personal and company's "dirty laundry" to yourself. Mentioning to a co-worker or customer that "the boss is never here," or "I'm about to get evicted from my apartment," or "my co-worker is incompetent" is not only unprofessional, but waves a big red flag to a customer who probably has enough problems without hearing about yours. That customer is likely to decide to do business elsewhere.

Disney has a saying: "It may not be your fault, but it's your problem." Ritz frequently reminds employees that: "You own it." Marketers refer to this as **lateral service,** which means every employee is to handle any customer issue that comes up, regardless of the employee's position in the firm. In addition, employees are expected to help co-workers who ask for help. And there's no need to keep score: "I've helped you 10 times this month and you've only helped me once." Things will even out over time.

In the end, when everyone lends a helping hand, it makes for a much better team atmosphere. Sports coaches often use the phrase, "TEAM stands for Together Everyone Achieves More." While a cliché, they are right. Getting the right people "on the bus" as author Jim Collins professed in his best seller, *Good to Great*, is so critical. But having everyone working together to drive the bus in the right direction is equally important.

THE MARKETING AND SALES LINK

As humans, we usually do things that benefit us—me, myself and I. Yes, some cultures are more collectivistic than others, but in today's world, people are pretty self-serving. Many firms particularly struggle with getting salespeople to be good team members or participating in what academics refer to as organizational citizenship behaviors. Why is this?

Well, most salespeople are going to do what they need to do to survive. If they are commission-based and don't sell, they don't eat. If they don't meet their quota, they will be looking for another job (involuntarily). So why not tie some of their compensation to things other than sales? While you don't want to pay your salespeople a pure salary—there goes their motivation—you can give them bonuses based on their willingness to do things they don't get direct compensation for, like being team players.

DO YOU BARK?

Brainstorm:
* Who is a business leader you admire? Why?

Assess:
* What kind of input do employees have in your training programs?

Rank:
* If you could fire one customer, who would it be?

Keys to Implement:

<u>Attack Dog Key to Defend Your Turf</u>:
Recognize one employee this month for being a great team player.

<u>Attack Dog Key to Hunt Your Prey</u>:
Fire one bad customer within the next six months.

CHAPTER 9
YOUR DOG AND PONY SHOW

Creating first-class promotional elements on a tight budget

JEB'S GEMS
    *   First Impressions
SCOTT'S STEPS
      *   The Basic Communication Model
      *   The Hierarchy of Effects
      *   Integrated Marketing Communication Tools
      *   The IMC Message
THE MARKETING AND SALES LINK
DO YOU BARK?

Why Is It? (aka The Advertising Poem)

*A man wakes up after sleeping under an advertised
blanket, on an advertised mattress,
pulls off advertised pajamas, bathes in an advertised shower,
shaves with an advertised razor, brushes his teeth with
advertised toothpaste, washes with advertised soap,*

puts on advertised clothes, drinks a cup of advertised coffee, drives to work in an advertised car, and then refuses to advertise, believing it doesn't pay. Later, when business is poor, he advertises it for sale. Why is it?

—A*NONYMOUS*

JEB'S GEMS
FIRST IMPRESSIONS

For any small business that sells a service, the "dog and pony show" is the first meeting with a new client.

That meeting, however, is not the first impression you make on your client.

In fact, that client has gotten in touch with you for a reason: Either she has seen your vans around her neighborhood, or noticed your ad in the local newspaper, or has received a direct-mail marketing promotion from your company, or has heard a good report about your work from a friend who hired you in the past.

Even when the client calls to say she might be interested in doing business with you, don't schedule a face-to-face meeting right away.

What we at JEB Design/Build do instead is take some time to "qualify" the client. Is she really looking for the kind of service that our business offers? Is her job big enough to be worth our while? Small enough to be manageable? Does she fit the "profile" of our ideal client?

Very often, we can tell from that first phone call if this is a customer worth spending our company's valuable time to pursue.

If we like the client and the client likes us during that phone call, it's still not time to meet. Even if that customer seems to perfectly fit our company's "ideal client profile," it's still not time.

So before we set up a first meeting, we send some information about our company and our process to this potential client's house. It's OK to follow up via e-mail, but we always send something through regular mail first. The material describes the kinds of jobs we do, shows pictures of our work and gives the customer a sense of whether she's "barking up the right tree," so to speak. It also shows the client that we're a "real" company that's organized and professional enough to follow a process and prepare useful materials.

At this point, the customer might decide against us, and that's OK; not everyone wants to deal with a "real" company. A "no" right here usually means her job wasn't the kind that our firm is looking for anyway.

But the client could decide to take the next step and meet with us. We find out which way she's leaning when one of our sales reps calls her a few days after the mailing goes out.

That first face-to-face meeting is where the customer will really judge us and decide whether to hire us.

Many of the remodelers and builders who come to me for sales and marketing advice have used a similar system with success. But it's just the preamble to the real dog-and-pony show: the first meeting.

Here are six keys to a successful one:

* Forget about selling. That's too abrupt for a first meeting. Remember being scared half to death every time you went to the dentist as a kid? He'd say, "Open your mouth," and then start drilling. Today's dentists don't do that. Before you open your mouth, your dentist probably explains what's about to happen and answers all of your questions. Likewise, that's a good way to spend your first meeting with a new client. Instead, explain your process. Let the client get to know you, your company and your process.
* Avoid meeting with just a husband or just a wife if both will be involved in the decision about whom to hire. Most people aren't going to make a major financial decision without his or her partner in the room.
* Don't expect to close the deal during the first meeting. This is the first of many meetings. Right now, your goal is to get the customer to say, "I like your company; I like your process."
* Be prepared to discuss any "better deals" that your competitors may have advertised or even offered to the potential client. When you respond, differentiate yourself from the competition by changing the dialogue. Explain that comparing contractors or businesses or service providers to each other by price alone is a little like comparing apples to oranges. Listen to what the client really wants, and you'll find that those needs probably revolve more around trust than around price.

* Listen attentively to the client's talk about physical things—the "bricks and sticks"—like which kind of floor tile she likes or how big she wants the breakfast nook to be. But steer the conversation away from the physical and toward the emotional. Find out what the customer is truly looking for in the experience. It's usually someone who is trustworthy, reliable, honest and capable.
* Take your time. Getting to and through the "emotional" part of that first in-person discussion could take a while. Schedule at least an hour and a half.

SCOTT'S STEPS
THE BASIC COMMUNICATION MODEL

In this chapter, we are going to discuss a concept called **Integrated Marketing Communication**, or IMC.

IMC used to be called "promotion," or the fourth "P" of marketing: Product, Price, Placement and Promotion. Today, we call it IMC because, for one, communication is much broader than promotion.

Everything a firm does says something about what it is as a company; you and your business communicate even when you're not doing it consciously. You can't *not* communicate as John Burnett and Sandra Moriarty advocated in their book, *Introduction to Marketing Communication: An Integrated Approach*.

From the vans that your employees drive, to the uniforms they wear, to your press releases and billboards, your company is conveying an image.

Integrating that image means making it consistent. Every piece of communication from a firm needs to have the same look and feel—to maintain its brand identity.

Before we discuss IMC in more detail, let's talk about the **basic communication model**, which is applicable whether two people are talking out on the street or if a firm is trying to communicate its differential advantage to consumers via TV advertising.

The model starts with a **sender** and **receiver**. In the case of marketing, the sender is the company and the receiver is the consumer. The message goes from the sender to the receiver via a **medium** like a TV ad, radio ad, billboard or coupon. Also, every model has "**noise**"—not just audible sounds, but anything that can distract the consumer from processing the message. With so many different marketing messages out there today, firms have to find a way to break through that clutter or noise.

Another part of the model is the **feedback loop,** where the receiver (the consumer) responds to the message. The consumer can give a response by responding to a survey, participating in a focus group, asking the firm for more information or even purchasing the product. Sometimes, the feedback can be instantaneous, as it is in the case of personal selling. In other cases, it may take several months for a company to "hear" the feedback, if it's coming from survey research about a TV ad campaign, for example.

The last two pieces of the model are the encoding and decoding gaps. **Encoding** is the creation of the message by the sender, while **decoding** is the interpretation of the message by the receiver.

How those gaps work: A company may want to create an ad that makes a product look sophisticated. Yet, if the business does not encode the ad properly, and the consumer decodes that the product is unsophisticated, then there is a gap or disconnect in the communication model.

THE HIERARCHY OF EFFECTS

The three main goals of IMC are to remind, inform and persuade, in that order.

Remind customers or make them aware of your product by getting your name out there over and over and over again. You may decide to use a jingle, a catchy slogan or an easy-to-remember phone number to aid in this process. Keep in mind that it does take time for consumers to become familiar with your brand. You can't simply run an ad a couple of times. In fact, in some of my research, it takes a consumer almost 10 times before he or she begins to recognize the brand via IMC.

Inform or educate your customers about what your brand does—once you've established some kind of brand awareness. Often, you can do this by providing customers with more information about your product or service's features and benefits.

Persuade or convince people to buy your product.

The three goals of IMC—remind, inform and persuade—work together as a process. This is often referred to as the **hierarchy of effects**. The ultimate goal is to get people to the persuasion stage, but the "remind" and "inform" stages are equally important. Take the supplemental insurance company, Aflac. A former student of mine is a sales rep there. According to him, the company has done a great job with its IMC to get people to the "remind" stage. A lot of people have heard of Aflac (when my former student wears his corporate lapel pin, strangers in the airport will shout out "Aflac" in their best duck voice).

The problem, though, is that most people didn't really understand what Aflac did or why they would need it. So Aflac was struggling to get people to the "inform" stage. Then, several years ago, the company decided to target those in charge of employee benefits at companies and to use their comical TV commercials to encourage potential customers to ask their HR representatives for more information.

The result: Aflac's U.S. revenue from premiums skyrocketed.

INTEGRATED MARKETING COMMUNICATION (IMC) TOOLS

Advertising can be very effective in developing a brand's image. But advertising, particularly TV ads, can be very expensive. Not only does an ad cost money to run, but creating and producing the ad can cost significant dollars, as well. Another challenge with advertising is that it can take longer to measure its impact than other IMC tools.

Television ads have value because you can show how the consumer can use the product. A TV ad also can entertain the consumer; just think about some of your favorite Super Bowl commercials. Still, the consumer cannot control the speed of the ad, so providing the right amount of information that consumers can process—at the right speed—is important.

The same is true with radio ads. In addition, consumers cannot see the product when you advertise it on the radio. Still, many companies simply strip out the video portion from a TV ad and use the ad's audio on the radio, which can hurt the effectiveness of the ad. Radio ads should be designed specifically for an audio-only format. If done right, radio ads work particularly well during commuter rush hours, when so many people are listening to the radio while driving.

With print ads, the consumer can control the "speed" of the ad; that is, he or she may read and view it as quickly or slowly as desired. That enables a firm to include more information than in a TV or radio ad. In a print ad, you still have to have a headline or picture to get the consumer's attention. If you open a newspaper or magazine today, you'll see a lot of ads, but the circulation of newspapers and magazines has been rapidly declining over the years. So your print ad has to grab the reader's attention quickly.

Outdoor advertising includes billboards, ads at bus stops, ads on buses and other material that you can strategically position so drivers can see it as they pass by. Having said that, my research has shown that eight words is the maximum that consumers can process as they speed past a billboard. Billboards—both in the traditional vinyl form and with the newer digital technology—are relatively inexpensive to produce. Still, the cost to rent a billboard has gone up over the years as cities have placed bans on new signs in an effort to protect skyline aesthetics.

Public Relations (PR) is about using the media to get your story told. Because you deliver your message through the news media, consumers often perceive the information from a public relations story as more credible than from a paid ad. A PR strategy can be effective in getting the attention of hard-to-reach consumers like company executives who may only read or watch specific media like the *Wall Street Journal* or CNBC.

Despite the positives, however, PR has its downside. For one, you can't control the story. You can write a press release exactly the way you would like it to appear in a newspaper or news site, but there's no guarantee that the media outlet will run your story at all or that a newspaper will print or a broadcaster will read it exactly as you have written it. You have to look at your story from the perspective of those in the newsroom.

For example, you might think a story about your company's new location would be interesting to everyone in town, but the journalists at the local TV station might not agree. For some good tips on public relations, check out former reporter Jeff Crilley's book, *Free Publicity*.

Like advertising, it is somewhat difficult to measure your firm's return on its PR investment, but it's possible.

Sales promotions include things like coupons, rebates, sweepstakes and buy-one-get-one-free specials. Companies run promotions because they are actionable and measurable. You can mail out 1,000 coupons to homes telling the recipients that they have seven days to redeem the offer for 20 percent off their next purchase at your business. Then, you can count how many people actually redeem the coupon within the seven days, and you will know if this was a successful promotion.

Direct marketing includes things like calling people at home (telemarketing), mailing them letters, flyers or packages, or e-mailing them. All three are effective because they can be targeted and personalized to the individual. Still, as we get tons of e-mails, calls at home and mail in our mailbox, it has become more and more difficult for any firm to break through the clutter. Some consumers prefer to see offers in writing rather than committing to anything via phone or e-mail.

Here are some tips for using direct marketing:

E-mail: This is not the same as "spamming." Contact only those people who have signed up for your company's e-mail newsletter or otherwise agreed to receive e-mails from you.

Telemarketing: Abide by the federal and state "Do Not Call" lists and rules. You might be subject to restrictions on whom you call and during which hours. And if a person contacts your firm to ask you to remove his or her name from your e-mail or phone-call lists, *immediately* purge all of your lists and databases of that name. Some people are very sensitive about this and get highly agitated by direct marketing. A misstep on your part could prompt an unhappy recipient of your marketing materials to write negative comments about your company online.

Sponsorship is about aligning your brand with another brand. The Dallas Cowboys obviously have a number of major sponsors: AT&T, Miller Lite, Bank of America and Ford, to name a few. These companies sponsor the Cowboys because they know the team has a loyal following. Cowboys fans are likely to buy the brands that are associated with their favorite team.

The good news for small businesses: You don't have to be a Fortune 500 firm to sponsor a team or event. Your company could win some local business by sponsoring a 5K fun run or buying equipment for a youth athletic team in your community. These contributions run as little as a few hundred dollars.

But do more than write a check or provide T-shirts with your logo on the back. Leverage or **activate** your sponsorship, no matter how little it costs. Ask if you can pay a little more to have a presence at the event, where you can set up a table, meet and greet people, hand out free samples or coupons and sign up people for your newsletter. At the very least, tell all of your customers that you are sponsoring this team or event.

Personal selling is interactive and personal. As the communication model shows, instant feedback from your customers about your product or service will help you sell it better. Using sales reps to personally sell the product puts your company in the position to hear that feedback and to immediately respond to it.

Of course, personal selling can be time-consuming and expensive because you have to hire, train and pay the sales reps. Also, some consumers have an aversion to salespeople. Some have had experiences with pushy or dishonest sales reps that will do whatever it takes to make the sale.

Train your sales staff to treat your company's customers better. The best salespeople make each sale in seven stages.

> Stage 1: **Generate leads**. The sales rep might compile a list of people who fit your company's target market. Hopefully, your IMC strategy will help you generate some leads, but you

can do it yourself. In his book, *The Power of Who!*, author Bob Beaudine, tells job seekers that they already know the people who will help them get a job. Instead of cold-calling or blindly networking, you can apply the same mantra to personal selling.

Stage 2: **Qualify leads.** To qualify a lead, the salesperson contacts the lead to see if he or she is truly interested in your product or service.

Stage 3: **Pre-approach.** This is when the salesperson gathers information on a prospective client.

Stage 4: **Approach.** Here, the sales rep really listens to what the prospect has to say and learns what the customer's needs are.

Stage 5: **Presentation.** Based on what the rep just heard the customer say, he or she can explain how your company's product or service might help them solve a problem or meet a need.

Stage 6: **Closing the sale.** Now, the sales rep asks the customer for his or her business. Closing the sale is one of the most difficult things for salespeople to do. It's human nature to have a fear of rejection. Still, in sales, you just have to ask.

Stage 7: **Follow-up.** Developing a relationship with your clients will lead them to purchase from you again in the future and to encourage others to do the same.

Regardless of what IMC tools you use (and I would recommend using several), I think it is important that you get creative. With so much marketing clutter out there, you have to have an advertisement or promotion that stands out. Author Jon Spoelstra provides a number of really good examples in his book *Marketing Outrageously*. Using rubber chickens in a direct mail promotion? It worked for him when he was with a NBA basketball team.

Managing your sales force well will help make your sales reps more successful. Three key things to look at with your sales force are:

Compensation. Determine how you will compensate your sales force: salary, commission or a combination? With a **salary**, the firm gets more teamwork from the sales staff, but with **commission,** you only pay people when they produce. Most companies use a mix of both.

Structure. You can assign your salespeople to work with specific areas, products, customers or steps in the sales process. With a geographical structure, someone has the east territory and someone has the west territory, for example. With a product line structure, one sales rep might be responsible for the sales of a specific product line and is expected to know everything about it. Another rep may be in charge of a separate product line. With a market structure, someone might sell only to the healthcare industry, while someone else sells to the teachers and trainers. Lastly, with a functional structure, different salespeople are responsible for the different stages of the sales process: One rep qualifies leads; another makes the presentation; a third closes the sale, for example.

Training. Whichever structure you choose, your reps need training to understand the company's goals, how they can meet them and what their incentives are. Training can be centralized, so everyone goes to the same classroom or location to hear a standardized message. Or training can be decentralized if new salespeople are assigned to shadow more senior reps in the field while they learn. Some companies combine centralized and decentralized training.

A hybrid of all of the other different IMC tools, **digital marketing** has the strengths of radio, TV and print, as you can include all of those media on a Web page. Still, too much information on a Web site can be a weakness of Internet marketing. Customers want to be able to find information quickly when they visit a site. They don't want to have to click on eight different links just to find a phone number. Web sites should be easy to find, easy to look at and easy to navigate.

Aside from your Web site, social media platforms like Facebook, Twitter, Instagram and others are great tools that make it easy for your business to connect with current and potential customers. Just as your marketing plan should include a blueprint for your advertising, direct mail and public relations efforts, it should include your social media plan, as well.

Simply setting up a Facebook page without freshening the content regularly, or impulsively tweeting without double-checking the message for accuracy, or posting questionable photos or wording that's too casual can backfire—especially if the message goes "viral."

Avoid the pain associated with the haphazard use of social media by creating a plan that outlines who will do the posting, when, and of what before starting out with Facebook or another social media site.

Also, keep in mind that social media is not a "cure all." It's most effective when you use it in combination with the more traditional IMC tools that we have discussed.

Who has one of the most popular Facebook pages? With over 100 million "Likes," Coke engages its customers with discussions and surveys on global initiatives such as eradicating poverty and gender equality. They don't just have a picture of a Coke can.

THE IMC MESSAGE

When you create an IMC message in an ad, a direct mail piece or on your Facebook page, make it clear: Does it tell people why they should buy from you? Does it explain your company's differential advantage? Is its overall look and feel consistent with your brand image?

You can communicate, or **execute**, your message with an **appeal**.

* A **rational appeal** is focused on facts and information, such as store hours, prices and product attributes or benefits.
* An **emotional appeal** is focused on emotions, such as sex appeal, humor and fear.

When deciding which medium to use for an ad, you need to determine:

* **Reach**. How many people might see the ad? If 1 million people watch a TV show you advertise on in a week, according to Nielsen, then the reach for your ad would be 1 million.
* **Frequency**. This is how often you run the ad. As we've discussed, consumers need to see an ad multiple times before they fully process the information.

* **Cost per person reached**. If you pay $100,000 for a full-page ad in a magazine with 100,000 subscribers each month, that ad costs $1 per person ($100,000 divided by 100,000 people = $1). If a different magazine charges $200,000 for a full-page ad and goes to 100,000 people, the cost per person is $2. Knowing the cost per person can help you decide in which magazine to advertise. Cost-per-person isn't the only criteria, though: Whichever magazine you select must be a "fit" with your target market. That magazine might not offer the lowest cost per person.

Regardless of which IMC strategy you choose, it's important to pre-test your materials. Once a direct-mail piece—or a coupon, newspaper ad or billboard—is out the door, it's too late to correct a mistake. And even though you can correct Facebook and Web page errors, you can't guarantee that people have not seen the incorrect post before you have a chance to change it. Run every IMC piece by your staff, friends and family—and even some customers, if you can—before publishing it.

To measure the effectiveness of your IMC after you have made it public, **evaluate** whether it was effective. To do that, survey some customers and potential customers to measure their **recall** and **recognition**.

Ask consumers to name some ads they have seen recently. If someone says, "Your billboard on I-49" without being prompted, that would indicate that your ad has strong recall. If you ask consumers which of your ads they have seen recently and they can't remember any, ask them about the billboard on I-49. If someone then says, "Oh yeah, I have seen that, now that you mention it," that's recognition. Recognition is positive, but not as strong as recall.

Other measures of IMC success include improved consumer attitudes toward the firm, intent to purchase from the firm and actual sales.

THE MARKETING AND SALES LINK

Keep in mind that the goals of IMC are to remind, inform and persuade—in that order. A lot of salespeople have a tendency to jump to the "persuasion" stage. Yet, staying "in front" of your customers with a phone call just to chat or with a customer appreciation dinner can remind them of you and your brand. Similarly, it is pretty inexpensive to create an e-mail newsletter that highlights new products and services. The key is to be consistent. Don't start a newsletter and then quit after a month. Similarly, you want to make sure that your message is consistent with your firm's message. In the end, keep in mind that your current customers need to be reminded and informed, not just persuaded.

DO YOU BARK?

Brainstorm:
* Take an ad that you like (preferably from another industry) and think about ways to adapt the ad style or execution to your firm.

Assess:
* Examine one of your IMC pieces (like a newspaper ad, direct mail piece or billboard). Is your differential advantage clear to the consumer?

Rank:
* What is the one IMC tool that you currently don't use?

Keys to Implement:

<u>Attack Dog Key to Defend Your Turf</u>:
Make your IMC budget 10 percent or more of your overall sales.

<u>Attack Dog Key to Hunt Your Prey</u>:
Double your IMC budget one month and measure the results.

CHAPTER 10
MEANER THAN A JUNKYARD DOG

The importance of sticking to your price

JEB'S GEMS
   *   Buyers Are Liars
SCOTT'S STEPS
   *   It's Easier to Lower a Price than Raise One
   *   Do You Truly Know Your Costs and Profits?
   *   Do You Know What Your Competition Charges?
   *   How Price Sensitive Are Your Customers?
   *   To Deal or Not To Deal?
   *   The Price/Quality Relationship
THE MARKETING AND SALES LINK
DO YOU BARK?

"The price of anything is the amount of life you exchange for it."

—HENRY DAVID THOREAU
AMERICAN WRITER AND PHILOSOPHER

JEB'S GEMS
BUYERS ARE LIARS

What do you say when you go into a store or showroom and the sales clerk asks, "May I help you?"

More than likely, you lie.

"No, thanks. I'm just looking," you say, even if you're going to a wedding that very evening and have to buy new shoes or you'll be attending in your stocking feet. You say it even if you have $1,000 worth of food in a broken freezer at home and need to replace the appliance today, or else.

You lie. I lie. Your clients lie.

It's such a pervasive practice that "buyers are liars" has become a common saying in the sales field.

Don't worry: You can still get to heaven if you lie to a salesperson. They're dirty, rotten scoundrels, after all. Right?

Remodelers and builders are in the business of selling products or services. So you know, as well as I do, that all salespeople are not scoundrels.

But some of your potential customers believe you're one, even though they have never met you.

They assume that when we tell them how much a product or service costs that we're trying to rip them off by overcharging them just to see if they'll be willing to overpay.

So no matter how well it's going with a customer on the phone or at your first in-person meeting, the moment of truth is when you bring up the price.

Customers always want it to cost less. Most think it *should* cost less. And once they're hit with "sticker shock," some will walk out the door. Try to stop them.

Seriously. Ask them not to leave. Ask for a chance to explain your price.

The fact is people who don't work in your business don't really know how much the product or service you're selling costs to make or provide. Most probably don't know how much the going rate is either.

Take the home-improvement industry. A husband and wife might walk into JEB Design/Build and say they have $12,000 to make over a master bathroom with a tiled shower, granite countertops, oak cabinets and state-of-the-art plumbing fixtures. My staff is well prepared for the underestimation, and gently informs the would-be buyers that such a package runs $25,000 or more.

That surprises most homeowners, who typically guess that their project will cost them about half of what it winds up costing.

The key to keeping that customer from walking out the door is your explanation, not only of how much each product costs, but of what the price covers: the product *plus* installation *plus* tear-out *plus* design *plus* service *plus* warranty. Twenty-five thousand dollars or more.

And if that's how much it's going to cost you to do the job—including your profit—then that's how much you should charge, no matter how forcefully the client tries to "talk you down."

A customer with sticker shock should never persuade you to lower your price. You need to charge enough to cover your costs—product, labor, overhead—*and* make a profit. The small business that compromises its profits every time a customer balks at a fair price is the small business that will be out of business within a few years.

The truth is that most small-business owners and managers—including most of the remodelers and builders I work with on their sales and marketing strategies—really don't know their true costs. And they're slowly going out of business—only they don't even know it because they're not paying attention to their numbers.

I tell those company owners: If you're going to go out of business anyway, cut your prices to the bone so your company will die a quicker death. There's no point in prolonging your misery.

In my opinion, you should never, ever, quote a price for your product or service until you know two things: 1. how much it costs you to provide it; and 2. how much you need to earn on this job to stay in business.

It doesn't necessarily matter what your competitors have quoted the same customer for the same job. That competitor is not going to do the job the same way you are, with the same quality, attention to detail, superior customer service and on-time guarantee—or whatever services you offer that make your business special and *worth the price you charge.*

Talk to your customers about value, which—if you're good—always exceeds price.

If the customer still insists that she can pay only $12,000, say, "Thank you" and "good-bye." Don't take on a client who can't or won't pay you a fair price for your work.

SCOTT'S STEPS
IT'S EASIER TO LOWER A PRICE THAN RAISE ONE

Pricing your product or service is one of the most important marketing decisions you can make. If you price it too low, you may be leaving money on the table; that is, you could have had a higher margin. If you price it too high, you might scare off some customers.

One thing is for sure: Changing a price after it is set is not easy. In fact, if you do have to change your price after it is set, remember that it is a lot easier to lower a price than to raise one. However, a drastic reduction in price can devalue your product or service to customers who have already purchased from you.

DO YOU TRULY KNOW YOUR COSTS AND PROFITS?

I've heard some business owners say that if they price a product below their costs, they can make it up in volume. Not sure what math they studied, but that's not true.

In some cases, you might want to have a **loss leader;** that is, you temporarily lower your price, maybe even below your cost, to bring people into your business with the hope that they will stay and spend more. Grocery stores often do this by selling two-liter bottles of Coke or Pepsi for just 99 cents during a sales promotion.

Still, the general rule is to price higher than your costs.

To do that, you need to know what your costs are, and not just make a "guesstimate." A friend of mine owned an orchard and an orange juice company. He told me that being off on his pricing by just a few pennies could hurt him on a bid to sell oranges to a school district.

The lesson: If you own or run a business, you have to learn basic **cost accounting.** Luckily, that's not nearly as daunting as it sounds.

The two basic categories of a company's expenses are fixed and variable. **Fixed expenses** are the costs that usually don't change, like rent, utility bills and the payment on a bank loan. If you don't sell a thing, you still have to pay these expenses. On the other hand, **variable** expenses fluctuate with sales; the cost of your raw materials is one example.

Understanding both your fixed and variable expenses is important, as they both factor into determining your **break-even point**. While it can be calculated in either units or dollars, the break-even point is what it takes to recoup your fixed expenses.

For example, let's say you start a Tex-Mex restaurant serving burritos, enchiladas and the like. You need to know how many entrees you have to sell before you get back to ground zero—or the break-even point. Now, do the math:

Break-Even Point = Fixed Expenses / (Unit Selling Price − Unit Variable Expenses)

The equation confirms that you need to know your fixed and variable expenses. Looking at the right side of the equation, you are calculating your profit margin on a per-product, or unit, basis. So if your average Tex-Mex entree is priced at $10, and it costs you $8 to make each plate on average (only taking your variable expenses into account), your profit per plate would be $2. Dividing your fixed expenses by your profit per plate gives you the number of meals that you need to sell to break even.

If your fixed expenses are $240,000 and your profit per plate is $2, then you need to sell 120,000 plates to break even (That's 10,000 entrees a month or approximately 329 a day if you are open seven days a week). Of course, you can raise your price per plate—if you can—and lower your expense per plate—if you can. Then, you would have to sell fewer plates to break even.

In the end, a simple break-even analysis can help you understand what your prices should be.

DO YOU KNOW WHAT YOUR COMPETITION CHARGES?

Business owners often think that researching their competition's prices is illegal. It's not.

Doing your homework to see where your prices are in relation to your competitor's is not only legal, it's smart. What's illegal is getting together with your competition to agree on prices in your market. That's called **price fixing** or **collusion,** and it can land you in jail. Just ask some Panasonic executives who were sentenced in 2013.

So of course, I do not advocate price fixing. Instead, find out if your prices are at the top, in the middle or at the bottom of the range of pricing in your market. If your prices are higher than most of the competition, that's fine if you can justify it with a better product or service, a more convenient location or some other special attribute or benefit—and if you let customers know the great value they are getting for the price.

HOW PRICE SENSITIVE ARE YOUR CUSTOMERS?

While the supply and demand curves of economics are beyond the scope of this book, understanding the basics of elasticity is important in setting your price.

In certain industries, a slight increase in price can result in a big decrease in demand. This is called **price elasticity.** A very inelastic demand curve indicates that people are going to buy the product regardless of its price. Of course, there are not many examples of this. On the other hand, a very elastic demand curve means people will switch to a competing or substitute product if prices go up.

If you are in a very elastic industry, then you need to continually find ways to cut expenses. Some companies keep their prices the same, but give the customer less and less (I call this "potato chip pricing"), but that's not the best strategy. A better one is to give customers more value for their dollar. We'll discuss strategies for this, like **bundling**, in the next section.

TO DEAL OR NOT TO DEAL?

Once you set a price, avoid changing it. However, you can offer discounts in the form of coupons, buy-one-get-one free or buy one and get free installation, for example. With these price promotions or deals, you are creating more value for the customer: **Value** is the benefit the customer receives in exchange for the cost. **Cost** is not just the money paid for the product or service, but the time and energy spent to get it: Did the client have to drive all over town in traffic to get a slightly cheaper price, for example?

Everybody likes a deal. Still, the sales promotion you offer must fit with your brand identity. A fine-dining restaurant, for example, should never offer coupons, even for slow nights.

Still, if your sales or discount periods are frequent and predictable, your customers will never agree to pay full price for your product or service; they'll just wait until the next sale to make their purchases. A lot of dry cleaners and pizza delivery places offer discounts so often that consumers ask the retailers to give them the coupon price even if they don't have a coupon. Bed Bath & Beyond has mailed out so many 20 percent-off coupons over the years that people just expect to get their bill reduced by that amount every time they visit—and the retailer is forced to accept all expired coupons no matter how out-of-date. Likewise, men's clothing retailer, Jos. A Bank runs so many "Buy One Suit, Get Two Free" or "Everything's 70 Percent Off" promotions that a customer would be foolish to ever pay full price.

Such deep discounts and frequent sales make customers wonder if the markups were unreasonable to begin with if they can cut prices by so much.

There's nothing wrong with bundling or other sales promotions, but use them sparingly.

THE PRICE/QUALITY RELATIONSHIP

The last thing to think about when pricing your product or service is the price/quality psychological relationship. That is, in some product categories, consumers believe that the higher the price, the better the quality.

This is a matter of perception or psychology—not necessarily fact. And it depends on the product or service category.

Let's look at electronics as an example. Even if every big-screen TV in a store were to come from the same factory, consumers often see a linear relationship between price and quality: The higher the price, the better the quality. The same is true in the wine industry. You might buy a cheap bottle of wine to drink at home, but when buying a bottle as a gift for your boss, you will probably err on the side of the higher price.

In the end, knowing how consumers perceive price versus quality is very important. It's OK to put a high price on a bottle of wine. You just have to let consumers know why; that is, explain your differential advantage. On the other hand, if your wine is priced relatively low, you have to let consumers know that it is still of acceptable quality.

A number of years ago, my colleague, University of Dallas Professor Sri Beldona, and I conducted some taste tests of different brands to investigate this phenomenon.

The experiment involved two national brands and two store brands (brands with the grocery store or retailer's name on them, also referred to as private labels) in the cola and cookie categories: Coca-Cola versus Safeway Select Cola, and Pepperidge Farm versus Safeway Select Chocolate Chip Cookies. The first result: In a blind taste test, people perceived the quality of the brands to be roughly the same.

Yet, before the taste test, the same people said they assumed the national brand would be of better quality.

Finally, another group of people tasted the products—but they knew what the brands were. Those respondents said they preferred the national brands over the store brands, but the gap was not as wide as it was on the paper survey that asked for perceptions without allowing the participants to taste the products.

The recommendation: The store brands should consider improving their packaging so it looks more like a national brand, and do more in-store tastings. In doing so, they can prove their quality to the customers.

Don't make pricing an afterthought. It takes a lot of analysis (e.g., cost accounting, break-even and competitor pricing) and psychology (e.g., price/quality relationship and consumer elasticity). If done right, it can lead to big margins for the firm. If mispriced, it can take years to correct.

THE MARKETING AND SALES LINK

Many veteran salespeople have told me that closing the sale is still the hardest part of the sales process. No one likes rejection, whether it's asking someone out on a date or asking potential clients for their business. For inexperienced salespeople, the close is particularly excruciating. They can talk about their product or service all day long, but they keep putting off the "ask." This is when you actually ask the customer to buy and you slide the pen and contract across the table. When a client does reject, the first reaction of the inexperienced salesperson is to lower the price. Yet, how do you know if price was the sticking point. And even if someone is concerned with the price, there are ways to emphasize the value the customer is receiving for the financial outlay. In the end, quickly lowering the price is an easy solution, but one that will make future sales with that client more difficult and hurt your brand equity.

DO YOU BARK?

Brainstorm:
* If you can't raise your price, what added value could you give customers?

Assess:
* What is your break-even?

Rank:
* Where do your prices rank in relation to your competitors'?

Keys to Implement:
<u>Attack Dog Key to Defend Your Turf</u>:
Cut your expenses by two percent a year.

<u>Attack Dog Key to Hunt Your Prey</u>:
Get rid of one price deal and add one new price deal each year.

CHAPTER 11
EVERY DOG HAS ITS DAY

Measuring success with the 'Bark-eting' Dashboard

JEB'S GEMS
    *   Count Your Money
SCOTT'S STEPS
    *   The Emergence of Marketing and Sales Analytics
    *   Did You Meet Your Objectives?
    *   Measure with Metrics
    *   Creating a Dashboard or Report Card
    *   Next Year's Objectives
THE MARKETING AND SALES LINK
DO YOU BARK?

> *"There are lies, damned lies and statistics."*
>
> —*MARK TWAIN*
> *AMERICAN WRITER*

JEB'S GEMS
COUNT YOUR MONEY

Talk to any truly successful small-business owner and one thing will be clear: He or she is obsessed with measuring stuff.

Profitable businesses measure costs, expenses, revenue, profits, quality, volume, sales leads—you name it. Then, they take all of that data into consideration whenever they make a move, whether it's selling, buying, hiring, relocating or pricing.

If you've heard the Kenny Rogers song, *The Gambler*, perhaps you believe the advice of the old guy in the box car who says, "You never count your money when you're sittin' at the table."

That's bad advice from an old gambler who was so broke he had to bum cigarettes from strangers and get around by hiding in a box car.

My advice: You'd darn well better count your money at the table, or you'll be as broke as the gambler in the song. You'd better count your money all day long.

You have to know where you stand before you can make your next move. You have to know how much money is coming in and going out; how much money you need to run your business and pay yourself. There's no way to know that without counting the money. There's no way to know that without measuring where every penny goes and where every dime comes from.

While you're counting, consider the quality of what you're measuring. You could have twice as many sales leads as you had last year, but are they leads for big jobs with high profits or for quick jobs that you can't charge as much?

If you count your money, you know which kinds of jobs earn you the greatest profits. If you are in the remodeling business, for instance, it's easy to see—from the numbers—that a room addition is more profitable than a kitchen. So if you have the opportunity to do both, but time only for one, choose the room addition.

Counting the money means you can follow the money.

I know what you're thinking: You didn't get into this business to sit around and count your money all day. You got into it because you love the craft of your field. You want to do creative work, or work with your hands, or spend your time advising your clients.

I do, too.

But you still need to send invoices, cash checks, pay bills and know whether you're charging enough to stay in business. If you don't, it won't be long before you can't afford to practice your craft.

You might believe that if you do work you love, and do it well, the business will take care of itself. My advice: If that's really how you feel, find an employer you can work for, because it's only a matter of time until the company you're trying to run will be out of business.

SCOTT'S STEPS
THE EMERGENCE OF MARKETING AND SALES ANALYTICS

Within the last five years, we've seen an emergence of marketing data. With expensive advertising campaigns and promotions, executives want to know their return on investment (ROI). Instead of managing by gut feel, today's marketers need to use data to make informed decisions.

Author Michael Lewis opened a lot of people's eyes to metric-based decision-making when he wrote the book *Moneyball,* which details how the Oakland A's, a small-budget baseball team, was able to win with relatively unknown players: players who fit the statistical profile that the team's general manager, Billy Beane, believed would translate into success on the field.

Mark Twain, as he noted in the quote that begins this chapter, believed that people over-relied on statistics to support their inherently weak arguments. I don't agree: Statistics have great value. That is, if calculated and used correctly, statistics should guide a firm's marketing decisions.

DID YOU MEET YOUR OBJECTIVES?

In Chapter 2, we discussed the importance of setting objectives that are Specific, Measureable, Attainable, Realistic and Time-Sensitive (SMART). While all five criteria are important, knowing how you will measure your objectives—even before you set them—is critical.

If you can't measure your objectives, how will you know if you have achieved them? Determining how you are going to measure your objectives, and when, early on is necessary.

MEASURE WITH METRICS

Call your measurements "analytics" or "metrics," but the key is the same: Make them objective and data-driven. Let's look at some key areas of marketing metrics:

Customer Service. The first key metric of customer service is **overall satisfaction**. Regardless of the scale used in a survey, every company's goal should be a high percentage—90 percent or greater.

Tied to that is the company's **customer retention rate,** or how many customers it lost. Many firms refer to this as "churn." You may acquire 100 new customers in a year, but if you lose 150 customers, you have negative **churn**, which prevents the business from growing.

Another metric that will shed some light on how your customer service effort is perceived is the number of customers who say they would recommend your company to their friends and family. Several years ago, consulting firm Bain & Co. introduced its **Net Promoter Score® (NPS)** to measure just this. On a scale from 0 to 10, consumers indicate their willingness to recommend. According to the NPS, those who give a company a score of 9 or 10 are actively promoting it to others. They call them "promoters." Those who give you a score from 0 to 6 are spreading negative word of mouth and are referred to as "detractors." Those who score the business a 7 or 8 are neutral or passive. To get your net score, subtract the percent of detractors from the percent of promoters.

Whether you use the NPS or create your own measurement tool, understanding what consumers think about your product or service is important. Customers might indicate that they are satisfied, but are not willing to recommend your business to others. What does that tell you? Maybe they purchase from you out of habit, or are simply too lazy to switch to another brand. Perhaps they are not as loyal as you thought.

Brand. As we discussed, brand identity leads to brand loyalty, which ultimately creates equity or value for the brand. So measuring each of these is important.

To determine **brand identity**, measure awareness. Ask people—even if they are not customers—if they have heard of your firm. While you can measure this yourself, many companies pay a research firm to conduct this sort of survey or they subscribe to a market study that gives the information.

Similarly, some firms use their market share percentage as a proxy for the strength of their brand. Your **market share** is the part of the market that you "own." If the dry cleaning industry in your town is a $2 million a year industry, for example, and you own a dry cleaner that does $200,000 a year in business, then your market share is 10 percent. Note that you can calculate market share in units or dollars. Because most small businesses are not publicly traded, you may have to "guestimate" the size of your market.

To measure **brand loyalty**, ask your current customers if they would recommend your company or product to a friend or family member as we've previously discussed. Or, you can also use internal data to learn how many of your customers have made repeat purchases from you. A more informal measurement that can gauge brand loyalty is the number of "Likes" on your Facebook page. While not scientific, keeping track of "Likes" will give you a general idea whether more or fewer people want to hear about and engage with your firm via Facebook.

Brand equity is the value of your brand. You can measure brand equity on a per unit basis. That is, how much more are consumers willing to pay for your product or service than for the average competitor's? That will tell you what kind of a price premium you are able to capture.

Similarly, if your market share in dollars exceeds your market share in units, you will know that you have a price premium and some kind of equity. While some companies have proprietary formulas to measure the equity of their large, multinational corporations, small businesses usually work with consultants to calculate the value of their brands.

This information can be very valuable, particularly if you plan to sell your business in the future. If you sell, you would want to negotiate a price for more than just the company's physical assets, as there is value in the brand that you have created.

Integrated Marketing Communication. The old adage, "I know that half of my advertising works. I just don't know which half," is still true today. And using a multi-pronged approach to IMC makes it even more difficult to gauge what is working.

In other words, if you use several IMC tools, like billboards, newspaper ads and direct mail, for example, it is difficult to gauge the success of each one individually. Seeing your billboard could remind a consumer to check out your Web site. In that case, which IMC tool worked: the billboard or the Web site? The answer may be both.

One way to measure the success of your advertising is to buy a bank of telephone numbers or Web site addresses (it's really not that expensive). Assign a different phone number or Web address to each direct mail piece and newspaper or radio ad, and then track how many sales you got from each.

You can create a simple metric for each of those IMC tools: Divide the amount you spent on radio ads by the number of sales you got from the ad. Do the same for every IMC tool so you can compare their success and determine which ones are most worth your money.

Web. The many metrics to measure your digital and social media efforts are beyond the scope of this book. Still, you can easily employ a few key Web metrics, like visits, unique visitors, click-throughs, time spent on each page and abandonment rate.

A goal of every company is to get as many people as possible to visit its Web site, and to spend some time on the site. The more time consumers spend on your site, the more they learn about your products, services and company, and that increases the chances that they will buy something from you, particularly if your site is designed for online commerce.

Not everyone does, though. A fairly new metric is the **abandonment rate,** which measures how many consumers visit your site, place an item in the shopping cart to purchase, begin the checkout process by entering personal and payment information, but then unexpectedly exit before submitting the order. Consumers often explain that companies are collecting more information than necessary, including a log-in name and password. Having to enter in pages of data to make a purchase, they complain, is too time-consuming and invasive.

A tip: Don't make it so tough for someone to spend their money at your online store.

Google, of course, is a world leader in all things Internet. Yet, most small-business owners don't know about the many great resources Google offers through its analytics division (www.google.com/analytics).

Google can provide you with all kinds of data, including content, mobile and advertising metrics, to name a few. Also, with Google AdWords, you can move your Web site up the list in the search engine results.

Of course, you can improve your ranking among search engine results yourself by frequently adding fresh content via blogs and accurate, specific keywords. Hiring a search engine optimization (SEO) expert is well worth the fee.

Sales metrics. At the end of the day, you've got to have sales. Sales metrics give you the bottom line.

Some simple sales metrics include:

Change in sales. You want sales to grow each quarter or year.

Sales per customer. You want to "upsell" your customers to get them to buy more or new products. Your customers already know who you are and are satisfied with the service, so why not tap them for additional business rather than spending the money to look for new ones?

Lead-to-close ratio. This is the percent of sales leads that are converted into actual sales. For example, if you had 1,000 leads last year and 50 resulted in sales, the lead-to-close ratio would be 20:1; that is 5 percent of your leads resulted in sales.

Marketing/sales return on investment. This last metric deals with how much you spend on marketing and sales—including sales personnel—and the return you are getting on these expenses. For example, if you have $2 million in revenue in a year, and you spend $200,000 on marketing and sales, then your **marketing/sales return on investment** would be 10:1 or 1,000 percent.

Of course, there is no guarantee that you will double your revenue if you double your marketing/sales spending. The key is to measure the ratio over time and experiment. Maybe you can devote a little more to marketing/sales in one quarter or cut back a little in another, and then measure how each of those moves affected your revenue.

CREATING A DASHBOARD OR REPORT CARD

All of this data can get overwhelming. So companies simplify it by displaying it graphically, on a "dashboard."

Like the dashboard in your car, a marketing dashboard should have easy-to-read gauges that monitor the most important metrics. In your car, you want to know your speed, amount of gas, RPM, battery life and oil pressure.

In your business, you might want to show the top five metrics that you want to monitor each quarter on your dashboard. You should share the dashboard with all of your employees.

Some companies create a "report card" instead of a dashboard to simplify the numbers. On a report card, you assign a grade to each objective. If the company met the objective, the "grade" is a B. If it exceeded the objective, the grade is 'A.' If it did not meet the objective, the grade would be C, D or F, depending how far off you were.

NEXT YEAR'S OBJECTIVES

I acknowledge that initially setting your objectives can be a "crap shoot." You may not know what to expect. The key is to just dive in and set your objectives.

After the first year, you should have a good feel for objectives that are SMART. Having said that, getting feedback from employees on the objectives is very important, as well. Do they feel like the objectives are SMART?

Overall, objectives and metrics are fluid and need to be continually revised. The problem with metrics is that managers spend more time "making the case" for why their industry, firm or department is different from everyone else's instead of using the firm's metrics to inform and motivate the entire corporate team.

Metrics should get the conversation started with regard to the different aspects of a firm's marketing. Let the numbers work for you. I've seen how impactful they can be whether it was calculating the economic impact of a major sports arena, measuring the media/Internet habits of older concert-goers for a multi-million dollar concert venue or even determining the satisfaction of Super Bowl XLV volunteers (in a study with my colleague University of Dallas Professor Rosemary Maellaro). When you have the numbers, it's a lot easier to make informed decisions.

But remember to share your metrics with your employees and get their input. When you do that, you can become an Attack Dog Marketer, defending your turf and hunting for prey.

THE MARKETING AND SALES LINK

As we mentioned previously in this chapter, the sales metrics are the most important. At the end of the day, you've got to make sales. Without them, there's no money for the company and ultimately no money for the sales staff.

However, the other metrics in customer service, branding, Web and IMC can help diagnose issues that may be affecting sales. For example, a low brand awareness indicator may mean that it will take your salespeople longer to let customers know about your brand. Similarly, your IMC and Web tools should be helping you make sales. However, if people don't decode your TV ad message as you intend or exit your website without spending much time, then it creates even more pressure on the sales staff to remind, inform and persuade customers themselves. And if customers purchase from you, but rate the service poorly (or worse yet, decline to recommend you to their friends and family), then post-purchase or sales follow-up issues need to be addressed.

With the right metrics, the sales team and management can work together to improve the sales process and increase sales.

DO YOU BARK?

Brainstorm:
* What is the best way to share your metrics with all employees?

Assess:
* What metrics do you measure currently?

Rank:
* What are the top five metrics you would like to see on your dashboard?

Keys to Implement:

<u>Attack Dog Key to Defend Your Turf</u>:
Calculate your customer churn this week.

<u>Attack Dog Key to Hunt Your Prey</u>:
Calculate your Net Promoter Score or equivalent in the next three months.

EPILOGUE
THAT DOG WILL HUNT

We hope you have enjoyed our book. As we mentioned in the Introduction, our aim was to make this a straightforward and easy-to-read guide that will actually help your small business.

As we've stressed throughout, if you have a plan, let others know about your plan, and then have everyone at your company follow it, you *will* see results. Jeb has been in business for over 30 years. Has the plan changed over time? Of course. But there was always a plan. Scott has worked with a lot of different companies (big and small). Some of them had good plans for their marketing. Some didn't. But he found that once a company put something on a piece of paper, it made it a lot easier to discuss and improve. Everyone had the same level of information.

In today's world, people have very little patience or time for anything. We get it. It's easier to text than write an e-mail. It's easier to write an e-mail than a memo. And no one wants to sit down and write an entire plan. But you have to start somewhere.

So bulleting out some of your main points on a piece of scratch paper is a start. Like the Nike slogan, you've got to "just do it."

In the South, there's an old phrase, "That dog won't hunt." It means that something doesn't make sense or is a bad idea. In our opinion, running a small business, or any business for that matter, without thinking about some aspect of your marketing every day, just doesn't make sense. If you make time to craft your marketing strategy, conduct research, develop your brand, enhance your customer service and evaluate your IMC tools, you will take your business to where you want it to be.

With an Attack Dog Marketing approach, your small business "will hunt."

Feel free to contact us at www.attackdogmarketing.com.